W9-ABM-869

WATERLOO HIGH SCHOOL LIBRARY
1464 INDUSTRY RD.
ATWATER. OHIO 44201

VIOLENCE AND THE MEDIA

GILDA BERGER

VIOLENCE

AND THE MEDIA

WATERLOO HIGH SCHOOL LIBRARY
1464 INDUSTRY RD.
ATWATER OHIO 44201

Franklin Watts ■ *New York* ■ *London* ■ *Toronto* ■ *Sydney* ■ *1989*

303.6
BER

Library of Congress Cataloging-in-Publication Data

Berger, Gilda.
Violence and the media / by Gilda Berger.
p. cm.
Bibliography: p.
Includes index.
Summary: Examines the role of violence in the history of the
United States and discusses the extent of the violence portrayed in
the mass media and its influence on the society as a whole.
ISBN 0-531-10808-2
1. Violence in mass media—United States.   2. Violence—United
States.   3. Mass media—Influence.   4. Mass media—Moral and ethical
aspects.   [1. Violence in mass media.   2. Mass media—Influence.
3. Mass media—Moral and ethical aspects.]   I. Title.
P96.V52U63   1989
303.6—dc20   89-31502   CIP   AC

Copyright © 1989 by Gilda Berger
All rights reserved
Printed in the United States of America
5   4   3   2   1

CONTENTS

VIOLENCE AND THE MEDIA

PREFACE

Most Americans keep up with the world through the media. We read the daily newspaper and as many magazines and books as we can. We watch television, enjoy tapes on the VCR, and sometimes attend the local movie theater. We tune in the radio for news and music and listen to the cassette player and to stereo recordings.

Here are just a few items gathered from the media in just one rather typical week:

Five railroad workers, apparently impaired by drugs, were found guilty of causing a train crash that killed or injured about a dozen people.

A statewide poll showed that teenagers often feel a strong hatred toward gays.

Officials from several large sports arenas had a meeting to discuss ways to control fighting among fans at football games.

A man being held in custody died of a neck injury after a police officer beat him severely with a nightstick.

An eight-year-old boy was shot to death in his classroom by a crazed female intruder.

Police figures show a rise in mob-related murders.

A business executive, during a bitter quarrel with his wife, fired a pistol and accidentally wounded his two-year-old daughter.

The so-called crime of the year on television took place on the popular show Knots Landing.

Among the new movies playing in local theaters were the action flick *Bulletproof;* the scary supernatural thriller *Lady in White; Above the Law,* dealing with a lawman who karate-chops a swath through gangsters; and *Colors,* a realistic drama about street-gang warfare in Los Angeles.

These were some of the stories that the media related within the space of a week. Not even mentioned in the media were the thousands of additional acts of murder, rape, family violence, assault, robbery, arson, and drunk-while-driving crashes from police reports throughout the country and the many riots and demonstrations that occur coast-to-coast all the time.

Incidents of violence are rampant. They may even be reaching epidemic proportions. No place is completely safe—not city streets nor the suburban stretches, not ghetto apartments nor spacious decorator-designed homes. Not even schools, hospitals, trains, buses, restaurants, stores, police stations, or churches appear to be immune to the effects of violent crime. Newspapers and magazines headline a frightening succession of hostile acts stemming from, among other causes, racial prejudice, gang warfare, and drug sales and use.

But what of the made-up horror that is also commonplace on television and in films and rock music? A great many forms of bizarre violence are widely available through the media, and these images come straight into our homes, where they are seen by people of all ages.

How do you think these accounts of violence, real and made up, affect us?

Media violence, some believe, promotes a fear of personal danger. Authorities in many cities claim that people hesitate to walk the streets at night or attend evening concerts or shows because they are afraid of being attacked or robbed getting to or from the event. Children are not allowed to play on the streets in certain neighborhoods. Many people avoid attending live sports events or rock concerts for fear of getting hurt by boisterous fans who go out of control.

Assassinations, hijackings, and daily crime have led to the presence of guards, gates, guns, locks, lights, and cameras in our streets and homes. Many houses are secured with elaborate devices. Motorists have to park in indoor garages, and guards patrol schools and housing projects. As a *New York Times* editorial recently said, "No brainwashing has been required to accomplish these transformations; only convenience, only fear."[1]

Such fear, many experts think, leads to an escalation in violence and a loss of innocence, confidence, and pride. The result? A diminished quality and style of life for everyone.

This book will explore violence in the media in an attempt to answer the following questions: What is the extent of violence in America? How much violence exists in the media? In what ways are violence and the media interrelated? Who decides how much violence will appear in the media? Who *should* decide?

Finally, this book leaves you with one very hard question, which only you can answer. How much violence are *you* willing to tolerate from the media, and at what point will you walk away from it?

CHAPTER

VIOLENCE IN AMERICA

- *From 1960 to 1988, crimes of violence increased 180 percent.*[1]

- *More than 22,000 men, women, and children die every year in handgun accidents, suicides, and murders.*[2]

- *Anti-Semitic incidents increased 12 percent in the year 1987 alone.*[3]

- *Compared to Japan, a person in the United States is six times more likely to be burglarized, ten times more likely to be murdered, and 208 times more likely to be robbed.*[4]

- *Homicide, rape, and robbery were four to nine times more frequent in the United States than in Western Europe.*[5]

- *Serious crimes in America increased in 1987 for the third straight year. Researchers forecast further increases as more and more young people move into the most crime-prone age group of fifteen to twenty-four.*[6]

Violence has been defined as the threat or use of force that results in injury, intimidation, or the destruction of property.[7] Included in the definition are a wide range of actions—murder, rape, robbery, assault, burglary, and so on.

As crime and fear pervade the country, sources of violence seem to surround us. We see, read about, and hear about violence every day in the media—newspapers, magazines, books, television, radio, movies, and records. Sometimes, we are at a loss to explain the reason for the violence and to know why it is so prevalent in our country. But a brief review of the history of violence in the United States should help us understand our own times a bit better.

OUR VIOLENT PAST

Traditionally, violence has played an important role in American history. Even the briefest survey highlights the bloodshed and violence that characterized America's growth and development as a nation. The noted English novelist D. H. Lawrence wrote of America, "Men murdered themselves into this democracy."[8]

During the turbulent 1960s, the National Commission on the Causes and Prevention of Violence was formed and later submitted a report. Included in the report was a brief survey of violence in American history. Referring to the patterns of crime, violence, and lawlessness that have occurred repeatedly since the colonies were first settled, the report indicated that violence in America is hardly a new phenomenon. All too often, Americans have resorted to violence to solve their problems. As the committee said: "Violence has been far more intrinsic to our past than we would like to think. . . . The patriot, the humanitarian, the nationalist, the pioneers, the landholder, the farmer, and the laborer have used violence as the means to a higher end."[9]

The colonists who settled the land had frequent and often bloody conflicts with the native American Indians. By 1646, the colonists had pushed the Indians back, founded new settlements, and spread out in all direc-

■ 14 ■

tions. Many young men and women came to America as indentured servants. They worked to repay the cost of their passage and received their own grants of land. But farmers, especially tobacco growers, wanted a steady supply of labor. A few blacks arrived in 1619, probably as indentured servants. But after 1660, planters began buying African slaves in large numbers. By 1760, people in all thirteen colonies owned slaves, though most slave owners lived south of Delaware.

At the same time, the American colonists set a high value on freedom. In fact, they became such strong individualists that they began to resent any interference from the British. British actions injured American pride. The Declaration of Independence emphasized people's natural right to change or overthrow any government that denied basic human rights. Some even cite the Declaration as a model for legitimizing violence.

Slavery as an institution grew strong during the early 1800s as cotton planting spread westward and became more profitable than ever before. Territorial expansion, improved transportation, industrial development, and reform movements led the United States to become a world power.

For years, there were few laws on the frontier. Pioneers living alone and hundreds of miles from courts of justice often took the law into their own hands. In the early days of this nation, each person depended on his own fists and deadly weapons. Bloody, even fatal, fights were not unusual. The revolver, knife, pitchfork, and ax were all used in rough fighting.

Lynching and vigilantism date back to at least the Revolutionary era. Lynching was the chief way of dealing with robbers and thieves. And citizens formed vigilance committees to deal swift punishment to persons considered guilty of crimes. Vigilantes, though, often the only force to preserve order in half-settled territories, sometimes mistakenly punished the innocent.

The years before the Civil War also saw a rash of religious violence, mostly Protestant attacks against Catholics. One of the worst of these occurred in Philadelphia, where twenty-four persons were killed and over a hundred wounded. In Charleston, Massachusetts, a group of nuns were attacked and their convent burned to the ground.

The tragic history of slavery and the subjugation of blacks has been a major source of violence in America. The antislavery movement in the mid-1800s resulted in rising hatred between the North and South. Intense anger and bitterness on both sides led to the outbreak of the bloody Civil War on April 12, 1861. The war took a huge toll in lives and property. Homes were burned, railroads were torn up, bridges were destroyed, and factories and wharves were smashed.

Afterward, "carpetbaggers" from the North took control of the Southern state governments. In response, many white Southerners joined organizations such as the Ku Klux Klan, which worked to restore control of state governments to Southern whites and intimidate blacks.

As the country grew, new factories needed workers, and labor problems resulted. At first, factory hands came from Northern farms and villages. But after 1840, workers came from other countries. Because of keen job competition, owners were able to pay very low wages. Workers began to form trade unions to protect themselves.

American life changed rapidly after the Civil War. More and more people moved to the cities. The war seemed to have corrupted American life. Scandals and thefts characterized many businesses. With the growth of industry and cities, there came urban crime and turmoil that grew "by leaps and bounds." [10]

People seemed to lose their faith in legal processes as the chief means to resolve social conflict. Murder and assassination became the order of the day, as workers struggled to eliminate abuses.

Settlers and government troops battled the Indians to clear the West for settlement. Crime flourished in the mining camps and isolated settlements. Drinking and gambling often led to fighting and killing. Bandits tempted by gold and silver followed and raided shipments going to California or to the East.

Disturbances arose over horses, cattle, and sheep. There was constant feuding between cattlemen and sheep owners and farmers. In 1890, cattlemen in Wyoming imported a trainload of gunmen to terrorize farmers.

Much violence centered around the so-called social bandits. Jesse and Frank James, Billy the Kid, and the Daltons were desperadoes (outlaws) who usually worked together in gangs and repeatedly robbed banks, trains, and stagecoaches throughout large areas. But because so many of the owners of banks, trains, and stagecoaches were unpopular, the criminals were often viewed more as heroes than as lawbreakers. These outlaws came to symbolize the individualism and vitality of the West, and many legends grew up around them. Sooner or later, most of them were shot or hanged.

The government report of 1969, mentioned earlier, also cites immigration as another source of American violence. The frontier, the report says, attracted the discontented and the dispossessed, the restive, and the ambitious from many lands. Problems arose in this country from the refusal of America's Anglo-Saxons to adjust to the upward strivings of successive waves of immigrants.

Heavy immigration resulted in friction between the more established groups and the newer groups. Persons in some communities resented immigrants whose customs, ideals, or traditions they did not understand or appreciate. There was often violence among competing racial and ethnic groups. The immigrants found it difficult to win acceptance. Often, they were not given the same legal rights or economic opportunities as persons who had lived in communities a longer time. The difficulties of assimilating wave after wave of immigrants added to the rising crime rate.

The late nineteenth century was marked by mob riots against the Irish and labor violence. The violence against union organizers often had a strong element of ethnic bigotry, especially in its early years. Old-stock Americans, who were the factory and farm owners and the foremen, fought the efforts of Slavic, Jewish, Italian, Hungarian, and other immigrants who were simply seeking to earn a living wage. Thirty-five were killed and hundreds wounded in the Carnegie Steel Plant strike in 1892. Two years later, 16,000 federal troops were used to quell disturbances from the Pullman (railroad) strike.

Around the turn of this century, the Ku Klux Klan was responsible for numerous acts of violence in America. Between 1882 and 1903, about 2,000 blacks were known to have been lynched by the Klan and its followers. Many Catholics and Jews were whipped, tortured, and murdered as well.

In the early 1900s, urban and organized crime increased markedly. Criminal gangs arose in New York and other large cities, some following the Italian Mafia traditions of organized crime. These included systematic killings to settle feuds, procuring money illicitly by means other than stealing, and using threats and extortion to establish control of communities.

The years between 1930 and 1960 are considered an era of relatively little violence. But the pattern changed in the 1960s. The increasing anxieties of contemporary life in the United States and the 50 percent increase in the number of fourteen- to twenty-four-year-olds in the population together contributed to a major crime rise in the 1960s and 1970s. From 1969 to 1983, the rate of crime rose nationally by 61 percent. Rape went up 82 percent; robbery 44 percent. The teenage homicide rate increased a staggering 232 percent from 1950. And in the mid to late sixties there was a wave of political assassinations— President John F. Kennedy and his brother, Senator Robert F. Kennedy, Martin Luther King, Jr., Malcolm X, and Medgar Evers.[11]

The study of history has pointed up the following conclusions: America has from its birth been a relatively violent nation. Rapid social change has produced different forms of violence; religious and ethnic prejudice have produced great bloodlettings. The American journalist Harrison Salisbury wrote: "It is in the American tradition to try to right wrongs by aggressive and violent means. . . . Thus, if we are to find a remedy for our Time of Troubles, we will have to seek it in ourselves—in the complex and difficult task of adjusting our wants, our needs, our aspirations, to one another."[12]

WHO ARE THE VIOLENT ONES?

Violent crimes are committed by persons in all walks of life. But there are overwhelming concentrations of violence in certain groups. For one, men are the main offenders; males account for 81 percent of all arrests. For another, violent criminals are most likely to be young, between the ages of fifteen and twenty-four. As many as 67 percent of those arrested for violent crimes are under twenty-five. And they are poor. Between 90 and 95 percent of violent crimes are committed by people in the deprived segments of society—the unemployed and those living below the poverty level.

The percentage of blacks who commit violent crimes is many times that of whites, about eleven times higher for assault and rape and about seventeen times higher for robbery and homicide. Blacks make up 12 percent of the population and yet account for 34 percent of all arrests. In part, this is because most crime is committed in cities, and a large proportion of the black population is confined to inner-city ghettos. It may also result from a disproportionate number of blacks being arrested.

Interestingly enough, except for robbery, violent criminals tend to victimize members of their own racial or ethnic group. In the latest police survey of homicide victims in New York City, 44.8 percent were black, 35.3 percent were Hispanic, and 18.2 percent were white.[13]

Crime today seems closely linked to the type of open

and mobile society we have developed. The tensions, frustrations, and temptations of day-to-day living may be largely caused by a society that values individual development over family and community. The major factors at work in our society include rapid social change and further urbanization. Rising expectations combined with a low level of achievement result in a vast increase in gun ownership and use. The 1981 Task Force on Violent Crime wrote: "Crimes committed by individuals using handguns represent a serious problem of violence in our nation." [14]

Social change often places a particularly heavy burden on children and an excessive amount of stress on their parents. Thirteen million children now live in single-parent homes. Fifty-nine percent of all children live in a home where both parents or the sole parent is working and the children are alone much of the time. These "latchkey kids" number about 7 million. Over 5,000 children are killed by their caretakers each year, a million teens run away from home, a million get pregnant, some 5,000 commit suicide, and 400,000 attempt to kill themselves. And untold thousands of children of all ages are verbally, emotionally, and physically abused in their homes. [15]

A government study found that almost 2.5 million teens between the ages of sixteen and nineteen were "disconnected from society" and alienated. It attributed this alienation to several factors, including the breakdown of the traditional family structure. The major areas of difficulty include epidemics of pregnancy, suicide, and drug and alcohol abuse. In California, the Governor's Task Force on Youth Gang Violence reported that an estimated 50,000 teens belong to gangs in the Los Angeles area alone. [16]

The 1960s National Commission on the Causes and Prevention of Violence summed up the causes of violence in America this way:

To be a young, poor, male; to be undereducated and without means of escape from an oppressive urban environment; to want what society claims is available (but mostly to others); to see around oneself illegitimate and often violent methods being used to achieve material success; and to observe others using these means with impunity—all this is to be burdened with an enormous set of influences that pull many toward crime and delinquency.[17]

OUR VIOLENT PRESENT

The violence in our lives, often glorified and commercially exploited in the mass media, falls into several distinct categories. Articles taken from various sources in the New York media in early 1988 provide graphic examples of the most common kinds of crimes. Among them are those that involve *unprovoked* attacks on victims.

The body of twenty-seven-year-old Geraldo Leiva was found in a construction lot. A thin rope was tied around his neck; a block of wood was wedged in his mouth. He had scratches and a broken nose and other signs of having fought with his assailant. His wallet, with no money, was on the ground nearby.[18]

Three days after Donna O'Connor turned twenty-six, her body was found, facedown, in a housing-project parking lot. She had been shot twice in the head. Drugs were found on her body. A police official said that Donna had probably witnessed a drug-related shooting just before she was killed.[19]

At one o'clock in the afternoon, two gunmen entered the Glamourama Unisex Salon, killed the manager and hairdresser, and fled in a waiting car. The three suspects apparently had come to firebomb the salon to settle a dispute. Two crude firebombs were found outside.[20]

By accident, Willy Lee Williams bumped into one of several men who were described as drug addicts. They argued and then the men attacked Williams, hitting him with bottles, sticks, and a garbage can. Mr. Williams's body was found lying in the street around the corner from his home.[21]

Three fifteen-year-old boys were shot and wounded when confronted by a group of youths who tried to rob them. The victims appeared to be unarmed and to have done nothing to instigate the confrontation. They were attacked after one boy refused to hand over his leather trenchcoat to a youth with a gun. The assailant shot him, removed the coat, and fired two more shots, hitting the boy in the chest and head.[22]

Fifteen-year-old Rod Matthews lured his classmate Shaun Ouillette into the woods and beat him to death with a baseball bat. When asked why, he said he wanted to know what it was like to kill someone.[23]

Angered because he had lost his job with the Postal Service, Patrick Henry Sherrill shot twenty people, killing fourteen, in the Edmond, Oklahoma, post office.[24]

Two homeless men were set on fire while they dozed under some newspaper in an isolated bus terminal. A couple of teenagers, who ignited the paper, were arrested shortly after the attack and charged with assault and arson.[25]

Many of the violent incidents that beset cities across the country are tied to the problems of homelessness, poverty, and racial tension. Cities are losing their white populations to the suburbs, and poor employment opportunities are contributing to a growing economic gap between whites and blacks. A drop in the tax base has left inner cities with budget problems at a time of increased demand for social services.

Hate crimes are crimes motivated by racial dislike and other forms of bigotry. A report prepared by the National Council of Churches called hate crimes "a cancer eating away at communities and social institutions." Claiming to have documented nearly 3,000 acts of bigoted violence against blacks, Jews, Asians, and homosexuals, the report places much of the blame on such far-right groups as the Ku Klux Klan, the neo-Nazis, and the Christian Identity movement. The report concludes that "a large spontaneous wave of homophobic violence appears to be sweeping the nation."[26]

There is increased concern over a reported tide of racial and ethnic violence, as evidenced by the following media-reported stories:

The so-called Howard Beach incident in Queens, New York, occurred after several black men walked into a predominantly white community because their car had broken down nearby. At first, the whites exchanged disparaging remarks with some of the blacks. Then, screaming racial slurs and brandishing a baseball bat, the whites chased Michael Griffiths, twenty-three, onto a parkway, where he was struck and killed by a passing car. Another black man, Cedric Sandiford, was severely beaten.[27]

Members of certain groups, such as The Order, the Ku Klux Klan, and the Posse Comitatus, were convicted and sentenced to long prison terms in 1986 and 1987 for a variety of serious crimes.[28]

In several U.S. cities gangs of young shaven-headed neo-Nazis known as "Skinheads" committed several serious acts of violence. In Chicago, for example, a gang rampaged through several Jewish neighborhoods one night, shattering windows and spray-painting swastikas.[29]

A series of violent attacks against immigrants from India and Pakistan erupted in New Jersey. The alleged assailants waged a "little war" in which they beat to death a bank manager and a doctor, assaulted an Indian driver, pulled an Indian woman along a street by her hair, sent a mail bomb to an Indian family, and scrawled graffiti on an Indian home and apartment block.[30]

Rev. Richard G. Butler, head of a neo-Nazi sect called Aryan Nations, which is based in northern Idaho, believes in a white homeland in the American West. Sect followers have been prosecuted for church bombings, bank robberies, murder, and other violent acts.[31]

Violence occurs in many classrooms throughout the nation day in and day out. Violence against teachers and students interrupts learning and makes teaching a less attractive career option. Our nation's schools endure an estimated thousand cases a year of vandalism, arson, robbery, weapons' possession, drug incidents, locker break-ins, assault, and disorderly conduct.[32]

Although the following examples are all from New York City, similar incidents occurred in Miami, Detroit, Chicago, and other cities, big and small, across the nation. Mediation is one way officials are trying to improve race relations within the schools. Elsewhere, officials call for immediate suspension and harsher punishments for pupils involved in school violence.

In December 1987, it was reported that weapons were commonly carried by students at Park West High School. The principal, Edward Morris, said that carrying weapons was not unique to Park West and was habitual among students. Violent incidents occurred between Puerto Rican and Dominican students on one side and black students on the other.[33]

A racial dispute broke out between class sessions at a large high school. Four white students were gathered on a stairway when Michael, a black, tried to push past. Tempers flaring, Charles, one of the whites, threatened Michael with a knife. Michael drew his own knife, but a friend pulled him back. Michael threatened to get Charles later. Charles reported the threat to the dean and said: "We're tired of blacks jumping whites."[34]

Four teachers were attacked by students in an outbreak of violence in the New York City schools in late May 1988. The weapons used in the assaults ranged from knives to guns to bombs.[35]

WATERLOO HIGH SCHOOL LIBRARY
1464 INDUSTRY RD.
ATWATER, OHIO 44201

Gang violence is on the rise in Los Angeles and several other cities of the nation. Among the gangs that have emerged in the last few years are crack gangs, with members carrying and using machine guns to intimidate would-be rivals. Innocent people have been accidentally maimed and killed when caught in the cross fire.

Seven members of an urban gang were found guilty of a series of grisly murders and kidnappings of their rivals or foes. The gang, which had terrorized one neighborhood for twenty years, tried to conceal the murders by dismembering and disposing of the bodies.[36]

Recent figures show that vigilante violence is a growing phenomenon in America. According to a recent survey by the National Rifle Association, 75 percent of the residents of Kentucky, Tennessee, Mississippi, and Alabama keep rifles in their homes, and 36 percent have handguns. Forty-two percent of all handgun murders in the United States occur in the South. But even in New England, an estimated 26 percent have rifles, and about 5 percent have handguns.[37]

Gun-law opponents, such as the National Rifle Association, say that the police alone cannot deal with criminals, who outnumber the police twenty to one. Gun-control advocates reply that those bearing guns, including the police, are more likely to become victims than those who are not armed.

In a well-publicized case, Bernhard Goetz shot four black teenagers on a subway train in 1984 because, he said, they attempted to rob him. Although Goetz was convicted of illegal gun possession, he was acquitted of attempted murder and assault charges.[38]

Florida leads the nation in violent crimes—including an average of 532 deaths a year from gunshot wounds alone. Legislators attempted to deal with the problem by easing restrictions on carrying a concealed pistol, knife, tear gas gun, or club. "The Wild West, Florida-style," said one national magazine headline, referring to the state's new gun law.[39]

In a town in central Florida, two boys were shot to death in separate accidents. An eight-year-old was shot in the head by a friend, two years older, who wanted to show off his father's pistol. In the other incident, a handgun that was removed from the family car by a five-year-old fired as his father tried to grab it from his hand.[40]

Four people, including a fourteen-year-old boy, were accused of fatally beating a man, Raymondo Carabello, who stole $20 from a woman in a New York City bakery as she was buying a birthday cake. In a neighborhood where vigilantism had become a way of life, a group of men chased and caught the robber. Then, as a crowd gathered, the group beat the man, resulting in his death.[41]

Police violence usually takes the form of incidents in which residents, most often blacks, are killed by police officers, usually white:

In Tyler, Texas, a town where blacks and whites usually keep to themselves, three white law-enforcement officers were charged with murder in the death of a black Louisiana truck driver. The three were accused of having beaten to death Loyal Garner, Jr., a thirty-four-year-old father of six, after they had arrested him on charges of drunken driving.[42]

Two white New York City police officers were indicted on charges that they assaulted two black men in a racially motivated street fight. The officers were accused of following the black men down a street after a dispute and of shouting racial slurs at them before physically attacking them.[43]

Dallas, Texas, was in an uproar in January 1988, after the slaying of a white police officer, John Glenn Chase. He was shot *three times in the face by Carl Dudley Williams, a homeless black man with a history of mental problems. Mr. Williams grabbed the cop's pistol and shot him in the face as a crowd looked on, some shouting, "Shoot him!" The attacker was then shot to death by two officers who arrived on the scene.*[44]

Jail violence is a matter of intense concern. To be sure, many barbaric conditions exist in state prisons across the country. Prisoners are often packed into hot, dirty cells, bored and idle, with little or no meaningful work to do. Brutality, rape, and even suicide are the frequent results of these awful conditions.[45]

Violence erupted in a large-city jail in February 1988, injuring six guards and six inmates. Guards' use of force against inmates had increased after the discovery of 300 homemade knives and other weapons by corrections officers. Inmates blamed the heightened tensions on overcrowding and unusually vigorous searches.[46]

A police sergeant was charged in January 1988 with torturing a drug suspect, Everton Evelyn, with an electronic stun gun after beating the man with the help of two other officers. The gun is 6 inches long, battery-operated, and can deliver a charge of up to 40,000 volts.[47]

In January 1988, four police officers stopped a black teacher as he returned home from a faculty meeting. When he resisted arrest, the police officers handcuffed and beat him. For three days, they held the teacher in jail before allowing him to make a phone call.[48]

Experts say that mass murders, crimes involving many victims at once, are rare but on the rise. "It's hard to make predictions about the future," says James Fox, a criminologist at Northeastern University in Boston. "But over the decades, there has definitely been an increase in this type of crime."

Since the 1970s, an estimated 4,000 Americans a year, half under the age of eighteen, are believed to have been murdered in multiple killings. Torture and mutilation frequently accompany such crimes, often with a sexually violent motive.[49] Notorious examples of single killers who have murdered a number of people include the Boston Strangler, who killed thirteen women, and Son of Sam, who murdered six people.

Fox says that factors such as the aging of the largest generation of Americans—the "baby-boomers," born in the quarter-century after World War II—and a growing sense of rootlessness may be responsible for the increase in mass killings. In 75 percent of the cases studied by Fox and his associate, Jack Levin, the victims knew their killer, who was almost always a white male. The killer was familiar with firearms. There was usually some precipitating event, such as the loss of a job, a divorce or marital separation, and a growing sense of isolation.

Of course, Fox and Levin warn, thousands of people fit the profile of a mass murderer, but only a very, very few commit mass murder. Nevertheless, depression, the high divorce rate, and the tremendous home and job mobility in this country can lead an occasional, already troubled individual to break down and go on a killing spree.

All of the violence we have described is connected with crimes of some sort. Yet the brutality affects more than the victims themselves. It affects family members and the larger community. Sometimes, too, the terrible results are further increased by the media, who glorify and exploit these happenings for their commercial advantage. Let us now consider the proper role of the media in relation to violence in America.

CHAPTER

THE MASS MEDIA
IN AMERICA

■ *An American infantryman in Vietnam, when asked about all the media people covering the war, said: "Cameras. That's all I see wherever I look. Sometimes, I'm not sure whether I'm a soldier or an extra in a bad movie."* [1]

■ *The name of Matthew Solomon became a household word after the story of how he killed his bride of two months dominated newscasts across the country.* [2]

■ *Soon after the media widely reported the killing of a young black man by a group of white teenagers in an all-white neighborhood within a large city, the number of violent, racially motivated acts doubled in that city.* [3]

■ *A TV movie on wife beating, called* The Burning Bed, *apparently triggered related violence in three separate cities. In Milwaukee, a man, fearing for his own life, doused his estranged wife with gasoline and threw a lighted match at her. In Quincy, Massachusetts, a husband was so enraged by the show that he beat his wife to death, later saying he wanted to get her before she got him. And in Chicago, a battered wife shot her husband right after watching* The Burning Bed. [4]

- *TV investigative reporter Geraldo Rivera, on* Murder: Live from Death Row, *interviewed murderers on death rows in Alabama, Texas, and Colorado and showed videotapes of famous killers in history. The program was the highest-rated syndicated special in 1988.*[5]

Most everyone agrees that the mass media influence what people know, think, and decide to do. Yet people hold different views on the extent of this influence. Whether in reporting the news or creating shows of fiction or fantasy, the radio, newspapers, magazines, books, films, and television are considered sources of violence. Critics say that the media glorify violence and spread violent messages throughout our culture.

Two important questions come up again and again when discussing the media in America. To what extent is the high level of violence in the media responsible for the rise of crime in America? And how much and what kind of controls, if any, should exist in relation to the media?

THE ROLE
OF THE MEDIA

The average American spends as much time with the mass media as with work. Some even devote more time to reading, watching, or receiving mass-media messages. Although the exact amount of time varies, most studies agree that the average person spends over 20 percent of his or her waking hours exposed to the media. This is more than twice the amount of time spent interacting with other people![6]

The media are generally believed to be the world's most powerful means of communication. They enable people to see and hear faraway events as they happen. They bring the world and events that occur in it, from celebrity interviews to full-scale, bloody war scenes, right into our living rooms and into our consciousness. The media clearly have an impact on our lives.

Given the fact that there is a lot of violence in the media, we need to consider how much that violence affects our emotions, behaviors, attitudes, and values. Does violence in the media give us the idea that this is a violent world? Does it desensitize us to violence, so that it takes more and more violence to shock us? Does it teach us that all we can do is accept violence and give the impression that we will suffer if we don't use violence to achieve our goals?

Defenders of depictions of violence in the media say that hostile and aggressive acts—namely murder, suicide, rape, and robbery—are always happening in the real world. Therefore, the images that appear in rock lyrics, newspapers, magazines, and so on, are merely raising our awareness of and reflecting what is going on in our society. As such, they do not affect our behavior one way or the other.

Opponents take the opposite view. They say the media not only tell us what other people are doing, they also present us with models of violent behavior. By showing us that violence is an acceptable part of human behavior, the media let us know that it is all right if we are violent, too.

Perhaps the real role of the media is somewhere between these two positions. The media may both reflect the values of society *and* help shape tastes and values. As Morris Janowitz, University of Chicago sociologist, said, "They are at the same time both cause and effect."[7]

MEDIA: MIRROR OF SOCIETY

As institutions of society, the various media reflect the views of its members, experts say. And large audiences, we know, are attracted by vivid, gory portrayals of violence. Thus, violent crimes, riots, civil disturbances, and terrorism are all favorite media topics.

The media is also said to reflect the view of industry

executives and advertising agencies, whose lives depend on selling media time, or buyers of media time, who look for big profits on their heavy outlays of money. In other words, the media are largely profit-making enterprises that operate on the theory that what sells is good.

Thus, since evil seems more apt to grab our attention than good, there is more reporting of the ugly and evil in our society than anything else. Take as an example the racial incident in Howard Beach, New York City. For over a year, newspaper and magazine stories and the nightly TV news reported repeatedly on the confrontation between blacks and whites on the night of December 22, 1986, that ended in tragedy. As a New York state senator said, "Howard Beach became a new catch phrase for racism. . . ."[8]

The media in reporting about the Howard Beach incident, one reporter commented, seemed intent on portraying the community as wholly evil. They ignored many of the good aspects of the situation, such as the fact that many residents roundly and vehemently condemned the violence and justifiably viewed the confrontation as an aberration. Instead, most everyone searched hard to get quotes from individuals willing to say something derogatory about blacks, whites, or Howard Beach.[9]

Many critics point out that vice, cruelty, and wickedness are nothing new; they have exerted a powerful lure since ancient times. "Violence partakes of evil, and evil has always been more interesting than good, unfortunately," says Richard Gilman, a professor at the Yale School of Drama. "Great sinners are generally more interesting than great saints." Dr. Gilman accepts the prevalence of violence in art and thinks it "useless" and "silly" to protest such kinds of expression.[10]

Robert Brustein, artistic director of the American Repertory Theater and director of the Loeb Drama Center at Harvard University, points out that drama has always reflected a world that is bloody and violent. He believes that all writers must write about what is happening and that apart from their occasional effects on mentally disturbed people, violent movies or plays do not cause violence in society; they simply reflect the violence that is there.

Moviemakers such as Martin Poll share the same outlook. "Film is about life, and violence is a part of life. Unless you're going to do totally escapist entertainment, you can't ignore the subject of violence today, because it is prevalent in our lives."[11]

In considering the portrayal of violence in the media, Robert Liebert, a professor of psychology at the State University of New York at Stony Brook, poses an interesting question: Which came first, violence in life or violence in the media? "In a violent society, there may be an appetite for violence, in which case the media wouldn't be the cause—they'd be the effect, simply reflecting back on us who we are and what we do." In other words, without our bent toward being a somewhat violent people, there would be a different kind of entertainment on television and the other media.

On television, news programs account for only 15 percent of the total programming.[12] Most TV fare tends toward drama. The producers of the news shows, in order to compete, strive to make the news as dramatic as the entertainment. The most important story of many newscasts is the police shootout, the riot, the demonstration, the suicide attempt, or something equally shocking. The violent event is always first because it's more exciting. It makes for a better show.

This approach has led some to charge that television news is not really news at all but entertainment. Former U.S. Attorney Rudolph Giuliani has accused TV of "overdramatizing and oversimplifying" crime news. TV presents crime almost like entertainment, Giuliani said, rather than dealing with issues or viewpoints on what causes crime and what can be done about the problems of crime.[13]

Most of the time the media try to reflect American values and interests. Yet, there is some evidence that certain attitudes and biases influence the actual selection of material and its presentation. Selected ideas then appear more factual and valid than material left out. Communications experts find that people tend to expose themselves to messages that agree with, or fit, their own interests and opinions. Thus, the common effect is for the media to strengthen their audiences' already existing attitudes.

Sydney H. Schanberg, a well-known newspaper columnist, questions the responsibility of the press in covering highly charged events. Take the Tawana Brawley episode, for example, a racial case that threatened to divide a community. In that incident, Brawley, a black teenager, claimed that she was sexually assaulted by a group of white men. "Should the press refrain from contributing to the divisions in the community?" Schanberg asks. Or, should they print "every wisp of gossip, every rumor, every inflammatory charge that surrounds the case—no matter how outrageous or absurd?"

According to Schanberg, the press must walk a fine line between confronting and challenging the system and making the situation worse. Of course, many editors and newscasters insist on reporting everything, regardless of consequences. Afraid of getting scooped, and eager to fill up their columns and the airwaves with news, they tell all, "even at the risk of setting fires," says Schanberg.[14]

A kind of reporting called "police blotter" journalism is known to attract and hold the attention of readers and viewers. For this reason, sensationalized stories are often run as part of a series and inserted into the nightly newscasts. These special features aim to attract audiences by dealing with such "hot" subjects as prostitution, pornography, child abuse, alcoholism, and drug addiction.

In recent years, for example, there have been more and more news stories on the sexual abuse of children.

No one is quite sure whether this means that more children are being sexually abused or that there is just more reporting of such abuse.

Even those who believe that the media holds up a mirror to events agree that both the press and the electronic media take a sensational approach to crime in the streets. By thus heightening the public's fear of crime, the media create the somewhat widespread belief that crime is engulfing society.

Some suggest that the media's coverage of crime does more than exaggerate reality. It actually distorts reality, they contend. By focusing on the occasional violent attacks on middle-class residents, for example, it ignores the much more common violent incidents in low-income neighborhoods. Rarely does the media make it clear that blacks are more than twice as likely to be victims of crime as whites are, or that blacks receive harsher punishments than whites for crimes of a similar nature.

Almost every day, television shows violent battles between opposing forces abroad, such as Israelis and Palestinians, black South Africans and the South African government, and Catholics and Protestants in Northern Ireland. But although these incidents of violence are presumably not made up, many critics charge that television doesn't always give a truly accurate picture of what is happening. For one thing, the very presence of cameras may lead the participants to create an incident or have a confrontation. For another, a TV camera may make an existing situation even worse, as those involved try to outdo each other in showing their bravery and devotion to a particular cause. And finally, by choosing what to show and what not to show, the TV cameras can win sympathy for one side or the other, thus distorting the reality of the situation.

The media-as-mirror argument that newscaster Robert MacNeil makes about TV can apply to the other media as well: "I think television . . . does put a premium on violence. It—television—likes violence. It is a principal staple of television news. . . . Violence makes good television, and it does in drama, and it does in television news. Now, that's not to say that all violence that appears on television is done in an irresponsible way. Violence is also news, and it's in human nature to be interested in violence when it occurs, and television caters to that interest in human nature, sometimes irresponsibly, sometimes responsibly."[15]

MEDIA:
MODEL FOR SOCIETY

The National Advisory Commission on Civil Disorders was formed in 1967 to determine what effect the mass media had on urban riots in the early 1960s. The media did not cause the riots, the commission concluded. But news reporting "helped shape people's attitudes towards riots." Some people who watched or read of riots in other cities later rioted themselves. "No doubt, in some cases, the knowledge or sight on a television screen of what had gone on elsewhere lowered inhibitions, kindled outrage or awakened a desire for excitement or loot—or simply passed the word," the commission said.[16]

Two years later, the National Commission on the Causes and Prevention of Violence made an even stronger point. "Violence on television encourages violent forms of behavior and fosters moral and social values about violence in daily life which are unacceptable in civilized society."[17]

Rev. Jerry Falwell's *Liberty Report* blames violence in the media for the deterioration in America's morals. Along with all the words and images that are widely available on the media, parents must compete with rock stars, TV actors, and movie idols to foster their children's character development. Falwell and others say that, in general, media stars promote nontraditional values, which many consider detrimental to family life.

Dr. David Pearl, of the National Institute of Mental Health, points out four ways in which television, for example, affects viewers' tendencies toward violence: Television provides how-to-do-it training. It can trigger violence that might otherwise have been repressed. It desensitizes viewers to occurrences of violence. And it increases viewer fearfulness.[18]

Some child psychologists say that the mass media contribute to child development through "symbolic modeling."[19] In a series of experiments on the symbolic modeling effects of media violence, a group of children watched a film of an adult dealing with frustration by kicking a "bo-bo doll." Later, when these children were frustrated by having their toys taken away, they kicked and punched more often than children who had seen a different film.

The research of Professor Neil Malamuth, chairman of communications studies at the University of California at Los Angeles, and Professor Edward Donnerstein, a psychologist at the Center for Communications Research at the University of Wisconsin, has shown that a steady diet of sexual violence in the media has caused some men to accept the idea that certain kinds of violence against women, such as rape, are acceptable. When exposed to films in which women are beaten, butchered, maimed, and raped, the men not only expressed less sympathy for the victims, they even approved of lesser penalties for rapists in imaginary rape trials.

Two studies published in the *New England Journal of Medicine* in September 1986 found specific links between television coverage of suicide in movies or news reports and an increased incidence of teenage suicide. Dr. David P. Phillips and Lundie L. Carstensen, researchers at the University of California at San Diego, released a study that found that the national rate of suicide among teenagers rises significantly just after TV news or feature stories about suicide. "One of the theories," Dr. Phillips said, "is that the publicized story gives others 'permission' to do the same thing. 'Gee [thinks the teen], I thought I was the only person who was feeling this bad. I don't feel like such an oddball. I'm not the only one who has ever thought of suicide.' "[20]

Research suggests that violence in the press or on television may inspire a susceptible person to imitation. Analysts noted, for example, an unusually large increase in criminal aggression following two major events: the assassination of President John F. Kennedy in 1963 and Richard Speck's murder of eight young nurses in 1966.

Although the evidence is not conclusive that violence in the media makes us become more violent, one thing is certain. On some level, media violence suggests that physical aggression is acceptable behavior in our society.

THE FIRST AMENDMENT

The First Amendment to the United States Constitution states:

> *Congress shall make no law respecting an establishment of religion, or prohibiting the free exercise thereof; or abridging the freedom of speech, or of the press; or the right of the people peaceably to assemble, and to petition the Government for a redress of grievances.*

Legal scholars differ sharply on the meaning and scope of the First Amendment. Free-speech absolutists, such as Supreme Court Justice William O. Douglas, believe that courts and legislatures should not abridge any form of expression, including the most overtly sexual or violent material.

In his dissenting opinion in *Roth* v. *United States*, Justice Douglas wrote that those who hold the absolutists' view on the First Amendment must fight the prohibiting of violence in the media. They take the same view, for example, as the Supreme Court did in *New York* v. *Ferber* (1982), a case involving child pornography. Although they condemn child abuse, prohibiting child pornography will do nothing to stop underlying crimes committed against the children. Even if proof were available to show that the materials did promote sexual violence, the absolutists oppose any restrictions on sexually explicit materials.

On the other side of the argument is Robert H. Bork, former judge of the U.S. Court of Appeals for the District of Columbia Circuit. He writes that those who say the First Amendment is absolute "must be reading 'speech' to mean total absence of governmental restraint." This interpretation is, in his view, "impossible."

> Is Congress forbidden to prohibit incitement to mutiny aboard a naval vessel engaged in action against an enemy, to prohibit shouted harangues from the visitors' gallery during its own deliberations or to provide any rules for decorum in federal courtrooms? Are the states forbidden, by the incorporation of the first amendment in the fourteenth, to punish the shouting of obscenities in the streets? [21]

No one, not the most obsessed absolutist, Bork says, takes any such position. Therefore, he concludes, the absolutist position must be abandoned, for it is nothing more than a play on words.

CURBING THE MEDIA
AND THE FIRST AMENDMENT

Since the times of the ancient Greeks, some scholars have held to the view that violence in art can be cathartic— that is, it can relieve tensions. They hold with the theory that violent representations in art serve a useful purpose. They bring out into the open the cruelty that seems to be basic to human beings and thereby get rid of it for a while, according to Harvard's Dr. Brustein.

Arguing that the media do not have any negative influence at all, some believe with Dr. Brustein that the media are neither model nor mirror of a violent society. The mass media, and especially television, they say, are not representative of reality. Most citizens are not sociopaths, although they view thousands of rapes and murders on television. The media have only as much power as the public allows. Viewers can turn off their sets, and subscribers can read other newspapers. The media exist only to entertain and inform the public, not to change anyone.

David Cronenberg, director of such horror films as *They Came From Within* (1976) and *The Brood* (1979), was asked whether the kinds of things people see in horror films have changed much over the years. He replied that he found the subject matter to be about constant. In films and horror literature as well, going back to the beginning of time, he thinks the basic material is the same: unconscious. Only style and fashion and censorship in both literature and film change, according to Cronenberg. And those changes are due to the incredible frustrations and anxieties and feelings common to people of every age.

In a free society, control over mass communications is exercised mainly through the self-restraint of those who manage the media. Government interference with media operators is incompatible with freedom. In newspapers and magazines, controls are put into effect by individual editors. Interestingly enough, editors rarely curb the writers' self-expression. Since 1922, in fact, no editor was ever expelled from the American Society of Newspaper Editors for the abridgement of free speech.

Even those who are most convinced that media violence is harmful cannot suggest a solution. Jack Valenti is president of the Motion Picture Association of America, which assigns ratings to films based on the levels of violence and obscenity. "I saw more violence on network news programs during the Vietnam War," said Valenti, "than I have seen in a lifetime."

"What are you going to do, shut the news off?" Mr. Valenti asked. "Where do you draw the line? A movie might jolt a psychotic into action—or somebody might jostle him on the subway. . . . Anything could set him off. We lose tens of thousands of people a year to automobile accidents. Should we ban the automobile? We don't even ban handguns, and look at all the people who are killed every year by handguns."[22]

Thus, opponents to censorship believe the media must exercise their own controls when reporting the news. Their difficult task in reporting the news is to establish a proper balance between information and entertainment. Suppose before a riot the media report rising tensions and anger. Then the riot erupts, and some critics will accuse the media of sparking the violence. But if the media ignore the early signs of trouble, others will blame them for failing to warn society of the threat.

In trying to defend violence in the arts, television executives often claim that they are just giving the audience what it wants. Dr. Brustein says that people are very bored and switch the dial seeking excitement. This leads television producers to resort to more and more violent devices in order to satisfy the viewers' hunger for sensation.

A question naturally arises as to whether or not society should ban movies that feature themes of death and destruction, which may lead people to emulate the violence depicted. But if we banned movies, critics say, we would have to ban books, stories, paintings, plays, operas, and any other works of art that deal with violence in any shape or form. "Down this path lies the end of culture and art as we know it," says Canadian newspaper columnist Walter Block.

But there is an even more basic objection to censorship and prior restraint on the depiction of violence. Human beings are creatures of free will, and people must be responsible for their own actions. Artistic works that portray violence are not to blame for the actions of those who choose to emulate them. Only the criminals themselves are to blame.

Attempts to curb the media invariably run afoul of the Constitution. "Any kind of government regulation which tried either to shift the time at which programs were aired, or which banned them altogether because of the fear that they would encourage aggressive action on the part of children, would be unconstitutional under the First Amendment," declared Thomas Krattenmaker, a constitutional scholar and professor of law at Georgetown University. Such regulation would be constitutional only if the government could show clearly that violence would immediately result from the viewing of such programs by children. And even so, the government may not deny adults the right to receive news, entertainment, or other similar speech protected by the First Amendment on the theory that it may harm children.

Another argument against such regulatory steps is that they would lead to a succession of other similar curbs ideologically opposed to democratic principles. "The threat to freedom of expression in the imposition of sanctions in such cases is a clear and direct one," says Floyd Abrams, an attorney who has specialized in cases involving the First Amendment. "Every artist, filmmaker, or author would have to consider before putting pen to paper what someone could say later on what the so-called effect of his expression was. Once they start importing into their creative efforts that kind of guesswork about how people might react to what they do, we would inevitably have a diminution of the vigor of public expression." According to Abrams and others, the price is not one that is worth paying—nor one that, as a purely legal matter, the First Amendment allows to be paid.[23]

Mr. Valenti, an official spokesman for the Hollywood film industry, concludes that Americans pay a price for a free society. Would people who clamor for the banning of violent shows find the Russian model attractive, where the state tells you what you can put on television, he wonders. The price for removing what some people find offensive is the surrender to the state or another authority of the right to make judgments about what should be banned.

Dr. Gerbner, dean of the Annenberg School of Communications at the University of Pennsylvania, and some others say that official censorship does not represent the only possible remedy for the current levels of media violence. "The question is not one of more censorship or less," Gerbner says. "The networks are 100 percent self-censored as it is. The question is, on whose behalf is this process operating? Right now it's on behalf of the advertisers who pay the bill to get the maximum audience at the minimum cost, and cater to every existing prejudice. The networks should be censoring themselves according to a different value system."[24]

Many think it unlikely that efforts aimed at controlling violence and pornography are going to lead to other kinds of censorship. In countries such as Sweden and New Zealand, where media ratings are more strict than in the United States, they point out, there has been no increase in political censorship.

Many experts in the arts and the media are now taking part in the debate about the dangers posed for children by violence in the media. All share the same concerns about the impact of media violence on the family, especially women and children. The question is how best to protect all of us. And on that issue, as you have read, there are conflicting views.

CHAPTER

3

NEWSPAPERS, MAGAZINES, AND BOOKS

■ *Constant news media coverage of the Palestinian uprising in the occupied territories of the West Bank and Gaza Strip is blamed for escalating the violence in these regions.*

■ *When a Japanese teenage rock singer jumped to her death from a high-floor window, the press spread the news. Over the next two weeks, seventeen youths committed suicide by leaping from tall buildings.[1]*

■ *The national magazine* Soldier of Fortune *was recently successfully sued for $9.4 million. The suit claimed that the magazine published a classified ad placed by a man who wanted to hire a killer to murder his wife.[2]*

■ *Law-enforcement officials have testified that people arrested for sexually abusing or murdering children often possess sexually explicit magazines and other pornographic materials.[3]*

■ *Reporters have said that Mark David Chapman was led to murder John Lennon, formerly of the Beatles singing group, by J. D. Salinger's* Catcher in the Rye. *The novel is believed to have become Chapman's script for murder.[4]*

■ *The macabre fantasy writings of H. P. Lovecraft have been linked to the deeds of brutal killer Charles Manson, who is said to have acted out Lovecraft's nightmarish fantasies.*[5]

As anyone who reads newspapers can tell, the favorite topic of the modern news media is violence—violent crimes, riots, civil disturbances, terrorism, and revolution. Editors believe that such material sells copies of their newspapers, magazines, and books. In truth, it probably does. But what is the impact of press sensationalism on the public?

NEWSPAPERS

In the United States, just about every adult reads a daily newspaper. In fact, people in the United States buy nearly 63 million newspapers every day.[6] Thus, newspapers are so much a part of our lives that most of us do not consider them anything wonderful. Yet the newspaper is a daily miracle.

The 1,657 daily papers represent many different views and appeal to a wide spectrum of beliefs. They cover a host of varying views on politics and government policy. And they portray a wide assortment of ethical standards.

Modern newspapers usually present readers with a distinct point of view. In so doing, the papers continually suggest ideas, beliefs, and ways of judging persons and events in our world. What we read in our daily paper influences our values and opinions. It also helps us form our attitudes toward the important issues of the day.

In early America, the press played a major part in shaping the society. To Thomas Jefferson, the press was the best means of "enlightening the mind of man and improving him as a rational, moral and social being."[7] Up to the early 1800s, American newspapers were the exclusive property of the privileged classes. Because they commonly sold for six cents, which was considered a lot of money in those days, they were too expensive for the poorer people. And because there was so much illiteracy, reading the papers was difficult or impossible for large segments of the population. The time was ripe for a newspaper for the masses.

The first truly popular newspapers, the so-called "penny papers," were started in the 1830s. They were easy to read, gave lots of lurid details in the crime reports, and, at a penny a copy, were cheap enough for almost everyone.

The penny papers led to many imitators. The most successful one was the *New York Sun*, founded in 1833 by Benjamin H. Day. The paper paid more attention to news that would entertain the masses than to politics. It was especially strong in human-interest stories. The first specialized reporter in American journalism was George Wisner on the *Sun*. He wrote a column, "Police Office," that gave readers a daily roundup of crime news. In 1835, James Gordon Bennett founded the *New York Herald*. It matched the *Sun* "crime for crime, sensation for sensation."[8]

Of course, not everyone liked the new journalism, as this quote from early in the nineteenth century shows: "The extensive circulation of newspapers is a sure criterion of the *mental* activity of the people of this country, but by no means of the advancement of moral principles and virtuous habits."[9]

By mid-century, sensationalism began to disappear from many papers. Nevertheless, a second penny-press movement started in the 1870s and early 1880s. This movement kept up the old tradition of glorifying crime and violence. According to one example reported in the *Kansas City Times* of 1872, three men on horses stole about $1,000 from the ticket seller at the Kansas City Fair. Reporter John N. Edwards wrote in the *Times* that the robbery was "so diabolically daring and so utterly in contempt of fear that *we are bound to admire it and revere its perpetrators*" (italics ours).[10]

From the end of the Civil War to the end of the nineteenth century, the press adapted to the new conditions of American life. Even more than before, the 1890s "offered a palliative of sin, sex and violence."[11]

William Randolph Hearst bought the *New York Journal* in 1895 and made his paper the model of what was called "yellow journalism." The most typical story in the Yellow Press at the turn of the century focused on crime and had sensational headlines. Here, for instance, are some typical headlines from the *New York Journal* of 1886: "Death Rides the Blast," "Love and Cold Poison," "Screaming for Mercy," "Baptized in Blood," "The Mysterious Murder of Bessie Little," "One Mad Blow Kills Child," "Startling Confession of a Wholesale Murderer Who Begs To Be Hanged."[12]

The end of World War I was followed by the start of the Roaring Twenties. It was a sensational decade—jazz and flappers, Prohibition, speakeasies, and gangsters. The new way of life was met with a new kind of newspaper, the tabloid—small size, small number of columns, many photos.

The first modern American tabloid, the *New York Daily News*, co-founded by Joseph M. Patterson, offered its primarily immigrant and blue-collar readers a steady diet of sex and crime. By 1924, the *News* had the largest daily circulation in New York City. Bank robberies, muggings, and rape-murders got extensive coverage.

Since then, newspaper circulation has been growing, and newspapers continue to be lucrative businesses showing handsome profits. In 1980, for example, the annual advertising income of newspapers in the United States was $15.6 billion. A typical medium-circulation newspaper makes a 23 percent profit each year.[13]

Many criticize today's media for catering to the public's fear of crime. To sell papers, the press may exaggerate the amount of crime in the streets. This increases the fear of crime that justifies crime coverage, which again increases fear, and so on. The press reports violence because violence sells newspapers, critics say. The press encourages violence because the violent seek the publicity newspapers provide.

Publishers are blamed for giving too much space to "soft" rather than "hard" news. They are accused of focusing on scandal and sensationalism rather than on the national and international events of historical interest.

The special interests of the media, many believe, hamper the way they report the news. Fifty-eight newspapers (including the *New York Times*, the *Washington Post*, the *Wall Street Journal* and the *Los Angeles Times*), fifty-nine magazines (including *Time* and *Newsweek*), and forty-one book and motion-picture companies (including Columbia Pictures and 20th Century Fox) are managed by just ten huge moneymaking corporations. And the evolving pattern seems to indicate an even greater concentration of ownership in the future. According to a recent survey of the industry, independent newspapers are being absorbed by large media companies at a rate of between fifty and sixty a year.[14]

As with any other moneymaking enterprise, the newspaper's first task is to show a profit for the owners. And, at least since the time of Benjamin Day and the penny press, the amount of violence reported in the papers has gone hand in glove with economic gain.

Although some complain that the newspapers fail to do enough to combat the violence in our society, others charge that they call too much attention to the violence around us. The one point on which everyone agrees is that violence is a permanent fixture in today's press.

MAGAZINES

Compared to newspapers, magazines generally are less affected by the special interests of the owners. Also, in the magazine field, there has always been a much greater diversity of ownership and content.

In America, magazines appeared after newspapers

were already on the scene. Newspapers were regarded as necessities, but magazines were considered a luxury. The first periodicals were published only after people had more money and more leisure time.

From the beginning, magazines were collections of different kinds of articles and probably developed from newspapers. The term comes from the French word *magasin*, meaning "storehouse." The first magazine published in the United States was the *American Magazine*, or *A Monthly View*, begun in 1741 in Philadelphia by Andrew Bradford. It was soon followed by Benjamin Franklin's *General Magazine* and many others.

Until the end of the eighteenth century, magazines struggled to survive. Then, with the expansion of the United States came a corresponding growth in magazines. From fewer than a hundred magazines in 1825, the number grew to at least six hundred by 1850. During this so-called golden age of magazines, people read general (often called consumer) magazines most, but a number of specialized magazines sprang up as well.

At the turn of the century, ten-cent magazines became the new mass-market product. A wide-variety of magazines retained their popularity until World War II. Then, in the 1950s, there was a trend toward specialized, single-subject magazines, since the general magazines could not compete with television.

Over the following years, a series of U.S. Supreme Court decisions opened the door for the production, distribution, and sale of sexually explicit magazines and similar publications. One of the outcomes was the opening of "adult" bookstores. Criminal elements moved in, especially in the distribution end of the business. This led in some cities to bookstore bombings by competitors and murders of some people who were producing, distributing, or selling these materials.

In October 1967, Congress authorized the establishment of a Commission on Pornography and Obscenity.

Among the many topics it studied was the effect of obscenity and pornography upon the public. The commission's basic conclusion was that there was no evidence that exposure to explicit sexual materials plays any role in delinquent or criminal behavior among youths or adolescents. The commission report also found that Americans differed widely in their attitudes on the effects of sexually explicit materials.

By the 1970s, the number of magazines that featured juveniles engaged in sexual activities or depicted the sexual abuse of children had increased rapidly. There were magazines that told readers how to get sexual pleasure from beating children and others that, among other things, offered advice on how to avoid going to jail for molesting juveniles.[15] Other publications discussed the joys of incest and how to lure children from playgrounds. Photographs showing children being whipped or abused in other ways were advertised for sale.

Many critics focus on pornography as leading directly to violent crimes. They cite evidence from crime and detective magazines which present "true" stories combining sex and violence. They give examples of "sexual tyranny" in the literature and suggest that the stories encourage violence against women. Andrea Dworkin in *Pornography: Men Possessing Women* (1980) insists that pornography not only depicts violence against women but is also responsible for such violence.[16]

The 1986 government Commission on Obscenity and Violence looked carefully at possible connections between obscene materials and examples of violence toward women and children. The report they issued speaks of "harms," both physical and psychological, caused by the manufacturers and by the consumers of sexually explicit pictures and print.

A long line of experimental research by Professors Neil Malamuth of U.C.L.A. and Edward Donnerstein at the University of Wisconsin produced evidence of a link between violent pornography and antisocial effects. Males who had been exposed to such material showed a greater acceptance of violence against females and were also more aggressive toward them.

Two psychiatrists classified 1,760 magazines according to the imagery of the cover photographs. The authors testified that bondage (binding or imprisoning the victim) and domination (establishing a master-slave relationship) imagery were most prevalent, appearing on 17 percent of the covers.

Another study analyzed nineteen detective magazines. The covers tended to juxtapose sexual images with images of violence, bondage, and domination. Sadistic imagery, most often with men inflicting pain on women, accounted for 28 percent of the covers. Bondage was depicted in 38 percent of the covers, with all the bound subjects being females.

The incidence of rape is shockingly high in this country. According to the book *Porno Plague,* many rapists and child molesters get their ideas from magazines such as *Playboy, Penthouse,* and *Hustler. Porno Plague* states that the reason "pornographers don't come through the door right now and slit your throats with a straight-edge razor is because they don't think they can get away with it—yet."[17]

Although those who favor suppression of pornography may believe that it leads to criminal activities, this has never been proved. As Harriet Pilpel wrote: "A victim with a sad tale of child abuse may say that his father read explicitly sexually arousing magazines, but so do thousands of other fathers who do not engage in child abuse." The factors always include more than a single element. Also, rape, child abuse, cruelty, and murder predated the arrival of sexually explicit magazines.[18]

In testimony before Attorney General Edwin Meese's Commission on Pornography, attorney Alan Dershowitz attacked the notion that words and images cause rape.

He said, "approximately 99.97 percent of *Playboy* and *Penthouse* readers did not commit rapes. That 3 out of 10,000 readers may have committed rapes . . . can be put into perspective when compared to the percentages of church-goers, Republicans, college fraternity brothers, musicians. . . ." As Dershowitz reminded the commission, "all cultural expressions—not just pornography—evoke unconscious responses."

BOOKS

The same debate over whether or not pornography adds risk to women's lives rages in the sphere of books. Experts disagree about the alleged dangerous effects of words and images in books. "No one has been raped by a book," a judge once said.[19] Nevertheless, the 1985 Attorney General's Commission on Pornography said that words and images are the causes of sexually motivated crimes.

Somewhere around 5,000 new "adult" titles are published each year. Incest, sadism, bondage and discipline, bestiality, and sexual acts involving children are the common themes that run through these books. Paperback books are often developed as part of a series, such as the one that includes *Siren Slavegirls, Tales of Terror, Incest Tales,* and *Forbidden Fantasies.* The books include very detailed descriptions of sex or violence and are often written on an elementary-grade reading level.

A study of bestselling fiction books from 1905 to 1988 in the United States reports that bestsellers are more violent now than ever before in American history. The trend is called unhealthy by such experts as Thomas Radecki, M.D., of the International Coalition Against Violent Entertainment (ICAVE).[20]

According to Dr. Radecki, the theme of sexual perversion first appeared on the bestseller list in 1955 with the novel *Lolita,* a book about a man who marries his twelve-year-old stepdaughter. The first bestseller mixing sex and violence was *The Chapman Report* in 1960, and the first horror and satanic bestseller was *Rosemary's Baby* in 1967, which was made into a popular Hollywood horror film.

The study claims that violence in bestsellers has increased by over 300 percent. In the last years of the study, sensationalistic, violent themes have become especially common. Seventy-two percent of bestsellers and 78 percent of paperback books featured violent themes. Spy novels, crime and detective stories, sword and sorcery tales, horror novels, war novels, cowboy novels, and science-fiction stories were virtually all focused on sensationalized violence. As Dr. Radecki told the press, modern American readers of popular fiction are entertaining themselves with more sadistic and gruesome material than any previous generation of human beings.

Dr. Arnold Goldstein, director for the Center for Research on Aggression at Syracuse University, agreed with the concerns of ICAVE. Research evidence, he feels, strongly suggests that these trends to violence in books both stimulate and reflect the ever higher levels of violence in our society. In his opinion, it is very unlikely that adult readers are unaffected by these subtle but harmful messages.

VIOLENT THEMES
AND CRIME

Some who oppose sexual violence in magazines and paperbacks have launched campaigns to "clean up" the book and magazine racks at local bookstores. In some cities, they have been successful. The stores either withdrew the targeted material or at least removed it from display.

Among the opponents of pornography is syndicated columnist Jack Anderson. Anderson attacks pornography on the grounds that "the pornography trade is controlled by organized crime." Phony names and dummy corporations seem to be in charge, says Anderson, but behind them are the crime bosses.

An incident involving the sexually explicit magazine *Screw* illustrates the power of the Mob in this aspect of the media. *Screw* reportedly was on the brink of financial disaster when Robert "Debe" Di Bernardo, a member of a Mafia family from northern New Jersey, stepped in as co-president. Overnight, the company came back to life, and in short order, film-processing labs and film-making enterprises were added to the magazine's activities.

Georgia's Mike Thevis is said to control the "biggest smut empire in the nation." He reputedly keeps together his vast holdings by such crimes as murder, bombing, arson, and extortion. Thevis's magazines and films are said to feature such sordid sexual activities as bondage, sadism, and bestiality. Eventually, he was tried and convicted for criminal activities in connection with his holdings.

Violence and terrorism are frequently associated with pornography and commercial sex. The large amounts of money to be made from pornography attract greedy and desperate men, such as Thevis, "who are as ready to use extortion and violence to capture and strengthen their control of the vice rackets as any Mafia chieftain or soldier."[21] Members of the Mob and other pornography racketeers were also the prime suspects in the shooting of *Hustler* magazine publisher Larry Flynt in March 1978.

A University of Southern California report links exposure to violent pornography with increased aggression. In its survey of child molesters, it found that 87 percent of the molesters of female children and 77 percent of the molesters of male children modeled their activities on pornography they had seen.

"Sadism is not an unusual phenomenon among the men who cruise the streets or advertise in magazines seeking children as sex partners," says policewoman Barbara Politt of the Los Angeles Police Department's Abused Children's Unit. "File cabinets in the Youth District at 6th District bulge with photos of children trussed in ropes, chains, or stocks, beaten with whips, cut with knives, or with their body orifices pierced by a bewildering variety of sexual devices."[22]

The University of Southern California study and Officer Politt's observations appear to contradict the President's Commission on Obscenity and Pornography report of 1970. The commission found that pornography had no significant effect on sex crimes. "Women do get raped and battered. . . . It remains absurd, however, to suppose that the suppression of the image can prevent the perpetuation of the deed."[23]

CENSORSHIP AND THE FIRST AMENDMENT

With the rise in sexually explicit and violent materials come increasing efforts to ban or censor these forms of expression and to make new laws against them. The fear of the effects of violence and pornography in printed material has led some people to suggest that we make an exception to the constitutional guarantee of freedom of speech and the press. But as a statement by the American Society of Journalists and Authors makes clear: "If we take that freedom away from one form of expression, we will threaten *all* forms."[24]

A leader of the antipornography organization Morality in America takes the opposite view. He told a reporter that the First Amendment ". . . does not give the people the right to choose to read pornographic material" and that "censorship is a way of life in America."[25]

Philosopher Fred Berger stated what he believes are the three necessary conditions that can justify censorship:

First, there must be strong evidence of *very* likely and serious harm.

Second, the harm must be closely and directly linked with the material being censored.

Third, it must be unlikely that further speech or expression can be used to effectively combat the harm.

Donald Mosher, psychologist, points out that none of these conditions are met by pornography. There is no strong evidence that the more pornography is available, the more sex crimes are committed against women and children. In fact, there is some evidence to the contrary.

In Denmark, starting in 1967, pornographic material, including child pornography, could be bought by anyone over age fifteen. From 1967 to 1973, the rate of child sexual assault dropped a full 67 percent. In West Germany, pornography was legalized in 1973. During the next eight years, sex offenses against children under age six dropped 60 percent.[26]

Also, Mosher and others say that pornography has not been linked to serious harms. And attitudes that were initially changed through exposure to pornography can be reversed. One of the explanations is that pornography provides an outlet for antisocial sexual impulses. It permits the person to experience in fantasy what he or she might have acted out—violently—with a victim.

Most of those who argue in favor of censoring the press cite the harmful effects of hard-core pornographic material on the public. They believe that removing pornography will reduce sexual abuse and violence. Opponents say that removing pornography is an opening wedge to repression—and will be no more effective than Prohibition was in stopping the American people from drinking.

Among consenting adults, the constitutional right to privacy includes the right to include or exclude pornography. Civil libertarians hold that any attack on that freedom is an attack on all freedoms.

In the past several years, an increasing number of bookstores have been involved in censorship incidents, according to Maxwell J. Lillienstein, legal counsel to the American Booksellers Association. Sex education books are often kept in a back room or under the counter. Popular novels, historical romances, and magazines such as

Playboy that deal explicitly with the subject of sex are restricted as well. "If freedom of expression, guaranteed by the First Amendment, is to have meaning," Lillienstein says, "books and magazines may not be banned or restricted in any way simply because they are offensive to some."[27]

"We might prefer a library or bookstore or lecture hall without *Mein Kampf* or the Grand Whoever of the Ku Klux Klan," writes Ellen Goodman. But a growing list of harmful expressions would inevitably strangle freedom of speech.

CHAPTER

TELEVISION AND VIOLENCE

- *An elderly woman is brutally murdered in an episode on Kojak.*

- *Tweety Bird is squashed flat under a speeding, careening car, only to jump up whole again a few seconds later.*

- *A crazed criminal punches out a young girl in* Hill Street Blues.

- *Time after time, the Flintstone cartoons show Wilma and Fred Flintstone fighting, often with great violence, and then making up.*

- *A television thriller deals with a killer in a small New England town who viciously strangles a number of women with a strand of wire.*[1]

Most of us see so much violence on television that we almost do not notice it any longer. Yet it is definitely there. Often, the music is discordant or nervous, and the people are hostile to one another. There is fighting, shooting, yelling, and beating. There may be shoving, stealing, or killing. Scary shows usually depict violence, as do most cartoons.

Over the past twenty-five years, researchers have been studying the effect of television violence on children and adults. No one has yet proved that any particular problem is due chiefly to television. Yet many think that we need to decrease television violence. According to the National Coalition on Television Violence (NCTV), 80 percent of Americans in general and 94 percent of American physicians are of this opinion.[2] See what you think.

VIEWERS AND TELEVISION

Of all the media, television receives the most attention from researchers because it is everywhere. It is present in practically every household in the United States. Television may be the most important outside influence on child development in our society, second only to the family. In one survey by Yankelovich, Skelly, and White, Inc., 76 percent of the people questioned agreed that "television has more influence on most children than the parents have."[3]

Americans of all ages spend an average of seven hours a day in front of the television set. Adults spend about 40 percent of their leisure time watching television. This places television viewing third, just behind sleep and work, in weekly hours spent by adults.[4]

Children spend even more time than adults watching television, about three to five hours daily, says the American Academy of Pediatrics. This is more time than they spend on any other single activity. Even children with light viewing habits—two and a half hours of viewing a day—will have spent more time in front of a television set by the time they are eighteen than in the classroom.[5]

Unlike other media, television is used fairly nonselectively. As a survey carried out by Temple University showed, more than half of the 2,279 children surveyed, ranging in age from seven to eleven, reported that they were allowed to watch *whenever* they wanted; more than one-third could watch *whatever* they wanted. Most parents wish to eliminate programs of crime, violence, and horror from their children's television diet, according to the Yankelovich, Skelly, and White survey. Yet only a tiny percentage believe that they can actually keep children from watching such programs.[6]

Many people doubt that they could possibly be affected by television violence. Yet studies show that the average person becomes more angry and irritable when watching television violence and experiences a change in mood for the better when the violence stops. Murders and rapes are likely to be more common, and people's general anxiety and tension higher, when they are watching violent programs. The amount of fighting and beatings around the home and in the world outside increases. And many criminals admit to having gotten their ideas from television.

Obviously, representatives of the television industry and some social scientists disagree. They believe that the antitelevision crusade is based on false arguments. They hold that television is being made the whipping boy for all of society's ills. In their judgment, there is no evidence of widespread social damage due to television.

VIOLENT CONTENT
IN TELEVISION

Professor George Gerbner (of the University of Pennsylvania) has developed a systematic way to measure the amount of violence in programs. Program evaluators watch the programs and note the rate of violence per program and per hour. They keep track of the main characters' involvement in violence—those who commit acts of violence and those who are the victims. Included are fighting, shooting, beating, and killing, as well as comic, cartoon, and accidental violence, and violence due to natural disasters.

According to Professor Gerbner, television programs are filled with depictions of violence. In his words, television is "violence raised to assembly-line efficiency."[7] This violence, he says, has a harmful effect on actions and attitudes. Although most everyone accepts Gerbner's figures, not everyone accepts his interpretation of the results.

Each year since 1967, Professor Gerbner and his staff have released official counts of the violent acts on a week of prime-time television. His report is labeled "Violence Index." A summary of the statistics from 1967 onwards shows that the incidence of violence in television has been going up. And the rate shows no sign of receding.

Gerbner's figures show that the early evening "family hour" (when most children are in the audience), had especially high rates of violence. Nearly nine out of every ten of these family hours contained some violence. The rate of violent incidents in 1986, nearly eight per hour, was the highest since 1967. Similarly, the percentage of major characters involved in violence, about seven out of ten, was the largest ever recorded. For the past nineteen years, sixteen violent acts, including two murders, occurred in each evening's prime-time programming.[8]

The amount of violence in children's weekend programming is also at a record level. Children in the last few years were exposed to twenty-one violent incidents during each hour of television on Saturday and Sunday mornings.[9] The rate of violent incidents in these programs, which are mostly cartoons, is typically more than three times the rate in prime time. Television cartoons, such as *Roadrunner*, *Bugs Bunny*, and *Popeye*, contain considerable violence.

Rarely does an hour go by on television without someone getting killed, says the National Coalition on Television Violence (NCTV). In addition to the expected violence in the crime and horror shows, 94 percent of children's cartoons have violent themes. Typically, the leading characters inflict violence on others, and violence is portrayed as a successful way to reach a goal.[10]

The number of television murders is staggering! On average, by age eighteen, a young person will see over 18,000 murders on television and will witness 80,000 murders and over 500,000 hostile acts in a lifetime of television viewing.[11]

Industry spokespeople believe that television violence is a highly successful way to attract a viewing audience. And they know that action, conflict, and suspense are the main factors that determine a program's popularity. But even they cannot prove that violence is necessary to a program's success. In fact, certain research findings indicate that there is little or no association between a television program's violent content and its popularity.

Nevertheless, the television industry continues to use violence in its programming. In the industry view, it is an easy, relatively inexpensive way to get people to tune in. Fights, car chases, shootouts, brutality, and sadistic violence are often-used gimmicks designed to capture and hold the viewers' attention. Media critic Eric Mink also holds that they require less originality and creative ability than writing less violent scripts.

The way in which television programs are developed has been described by Richard M. Powers, chairman of the Writers' Guild of America:

> The network programmers let it be known what they're looking for. . . . The writer or writer-producer comes in with a format which is quickly reduced to the lowest common denominator by the network people—something like a group of men with large feet stamping out a grass fire. What is left generally is a series about two cops with a warm, human, caring relationship toward one another, leaving behind them—as they work their warm and caring way through the TV season—a mountain of dead bodies. In other words, the format is a vacuum—which must be filled by violence.[12]

Most of the opinions held by opponents of televised violence are based on federal government and academic studies. The first major federal research project was concluded in 1972. In its final report to the surgeon general, it did mention some slight relationship between televised violence and violent behavior in real life. But it went on to state, "Television is only one of the many factors which in time may precede aggressive behavior." And it added that children may indeed be made more aggressive by seeing acts of violence on television, but only if they already have aggressive tendencies.[13]

When Surgeon General Dr. Jesse Leonard Steinfeld was asked to spell out the conclusions, though, he stated: ". . . It is clear to me that the causal relationship between televised violence and anti-social behavior is sufficient to warrant appropriate and immediate remedial action."

Apparently, though, Dr. Steinfeld's statement was not sufficient to overcome the earlier implication that television violence caused "little harm." Government officials decided to commission a new research study.

A National Institute of Mental Health (NIMH) project reviewed over 2,500 studies on television violence and behavior that were done over the ten years following the surgeon general's report. It was entitled *Television and Behavior: Ten Years of Scientific Progress and Implications for the Eighties*. The NIMH concluded that violence on television does indeed lead to violent behavior in real life. It wrote: "According to many researchers, the evidence . . . seems overwhelming that televised violence and aggression are positively correlated in children."[14]

An independent evaluation was commissioned by the National Academy of Sciences. The academy concluded that the evidence cited in the surgeon general's report was insufficient to justify passing any new law or regulation. It also criticized the report for scientific shortcomings and for dealing with mild forms of aggression among children, not with criminal behavior.[15]

Most everyone agrees that antisocial, aggressive people tend to watch television programs with violent content. Yet, the evidence has not yet made it clear whether watching causes aggression or whether normally aggressive people just tend to watch violent programs. The research studies used to examine the effects of violence on television are generally of four basic kinds:

Longitudinal survey studies. They measure the effects of television viewing on the same people over a period of time.

Field studies. They collect data on people's normal viewing habits and behavior patterns.

Laboratory studies. They run experiments that compare the behavior of people who have just witnessed a violent television portrayal with the behavior of those who have not, to observe the effects of the television viewing.

Time-series studies. They examine the relationships between particular acts of violence shown on television and the frequency of similar acts in real life.

Both opponents and defenders of television violence use the results of these various kinds of studies to support their positions on this issue.

OPPONENTS OF
TELEVISION VIOLENCE

The National Coalition on Television Violence estimates that probably 25 to 50 percent of the violence in our society comes from the culture and gets reinforced daily by violent entertainment. Considering the 300 to 500 percent increase in violence in our society in the past thirty years, NCTV's contentions are certainly reasonable.[16] Violence in the United States started escalating around the year 1956, the same year the violence content of television showed a marked increase.

One large-scale 1978 field study looked at the relationship between televised violence and "real-world" violence. This study, which surveyed 1,655 London males between the ages of twelve and seventeen, found that boys who watched a great deal of television violence showed 49 percent more violent and antisocial behavior than those who watched less. The findings have been used to support the argument that violent television content creates an accepting attitude toward violence and encourages highly aggressive behavior.

Professor Leonard Eron is the author of a particularly significant longitudinal study on the subject. He started by interviewing 875 third-graders in 1960. Ten years later, in 1970, he interviewed the 427 he was able to locate. And he was able to track down 409 of the original group for a third meeting in 1981.

Professor Eron's major finding was that excessive television violence viewing in children is a cause of increased aggression. As he reported, male subjects who were seen as more aggressive at age eight rated themselves as more aggressive at age thirty. These men were rated by their wives as more aggressive, had more convictions by the criminal justice system, committed more serious crimes, and had more moving traffic violations and more convictions for driving while intoxicated.[17]

Other figures showed that 25 percent of the nine-year-olds who watched the most television violence in 1960 were convicted of criminal offenses 150 percent more often than the other 75 percent. Eron is fully aware that not all the crime was due to violence. But he holds that "a diet of television violence was still the best predictor of convictions for juvenile delinquency."

A sidelight on Eron's study was his discovery that parents frequently exposed to violent entertainment are more likely to physically abuse their children. Also, he concluded that growing up in such a family leads to the likelihood of future problems with violence.

Children who watch violence on television and see one child hurting another are *much less likely* to try to stop the violence than those who do not watch television violence. Violence comes to be accepted, if not condoned. There is a numbing of any feelings of horror, grief, or revulsion. Exposure to television violence over a period of time leads to a kind of deadened reaction. Some fear that this phenomenon, which is labeled the desensitization effect, may have considerable long-range antisocial consequences.

The Yale Television Center reports differences between heavy and light patterns of television watching. In an ongoing study of about 350 preschoolers, the most aggressive children (those who hit another child or destroy property) are the heaviest viewers of superhero cartoons. Children who habitually watch television play less imaginatively than light television viewers. The heavy viewers run around shouting the names of the superhero television characters but rarely extend ideas into make-believe games with story line and plot. Many of them are aggressive and use their "superlegs" or "superarms" to strike other children.[18]

Researchers at the Annenberg School of Communications of the University of Pennsylvania add another insight. Exposure to violence, in addition to inciting violence and often desensitizing viewers, creates the impression that we live in a mean and dangerous world. This impression gives rise to a sense of danger, mistrust, and dependence. Despite its supposedly entertaining nature, television creates alienation and gloom.

Dr. Gerbner and his collaborators at Annenberg release annual reports, called Cultivation Analyses, that focus on the relationship between the number of viewing hours and the extent of viewers' misperceptions of reality. The analyses are so named because of the belief that television violence "cultivates" feelings of victimization among viewers.

Based on these analyses, the NCTV concludes that heavy viewers are more likely to find the world a frightening place in which to live. Heavy viewers are more likely than light viewers to express the feeling of living in a gloomy world and are also more likely to have bought new locks, watchdogs, and guns for protection.

Since distorted perceptions of others and the world in general seem to accompany heavy television viewing, high-violence television viewers show an exaggerated, unrealistic fear of crime and violence. Witnessing television violence makes some people scared rather than aggressive.

The emphasis on violence in the world of television, they have found, affects one's ideas about the risks of being hurt in the real world. This includes encountering violence in one's own neighborhood, falling victim to violence, and feeling insecure in personal and group relationships. The result, they say, is to make those who are lower in status feel weaker, more vulnerable, and more easily controlled.

The sense of danger, feeling of vulnerability, and general uneasiness that are absorbed from the medium have some harmful side effects. They encourage aggression, exploitation, and repression. Fearful people are more easily manipulated and controlled and more susceptible to seeking simple solutions to complex problems. Fear may lead to rigid beliefs, both in the political and religious spheres. Such people may accept and even welcome repression if it promises to relieve their insecurities and other anxieties. That is what Gerbner sees as the deeper problem of violence-laden television.[19]

In line with the so-called mean-world syndrome, watching a lot of television is believed to lead viewers to assume that:

1. Most people are just looking out for themselves.

2. You can't be too careful in dealing with people.

3. Most people will take advantage of you if they get a chance.

The reactions to television violence can be intensified under certain conditions. Viewers may be worked up to a so-called arousal state by fast-paced action and a high-pitch level of voices and music. Such viewers are more likely than nonaroused persons to react to televised violence by behaving violently themselves. Researchers at Yale University found that children aroused by high-impact television programs showed more than average amounts of aggression.[20]

Many experts used to believe that television violence is a catharsis. That is, it redirects hostile violent energy toward safe targets or "drains it off" by means of empathetic experiences. This position, however, is not supported by some current research findings. Certain research has shown that people who watch violence presented as "justified," such as police using violence against criminals or members of the public using violence in self-defense, show a greater likelihood of using violence themselves.

One example came in October 1973, when a film called *Fuzz* on the ABC-TV network showed hoodlums in Boston burning derelicts to death for fun. Several days later, six youths in New York City poured gasoline over a twenty-four-year-old homeless woman and burned her to death.[21]

The most widely accepted theory linking televised violence with real-world violence, and one with considerable scientific support, is the so-called social learning theory. According to this idea, children learn appropriate behavior by imitating the behavior of adults and develop their value system by listening to what adults say and watching what they do. The popular television characters, therefore, are crucial role models for children.

The answers to the following questions can give a good estimate of the model's influence on children: How do these characters relate to one another? Do they use violent means to settle their differences or achieve their goals? Do they show care and concern for victims of violence? Is violence depicted so frequently that young viewers are desensitized?

Even more specifically, children learn by observing the rewards and punishments meted out to those around them. They quickly learn to repeat behavior that earns them praise and acceptance. If it appears on television, they may reason, it probably meets with the approval of the adult world and society in general. In many cases, it can strengthen the conviction that violence and aggression are sometimes permissible.

Heroes who resort to violence send a particularly powerful message to young people, since their violent acts are usually for a good cause, and they are not usually punished. All too often, the television hero wins success, fame, and love because his or her violent actions are more effective than those of rivals.

Television crime shows often follow a formula that uses standard, type-cast victims, victimizers, and defenders. One way social scientists study violence on television is by calculating the ratio of victimizers to victims. This produces a so-called risk ratio.

For every ten male characters on prime-time network television who commit violence, there are eleven who fall victim to it. But for every ten female perpetrators of violence, there are sixteen female victims. Females who are young and beautiful are the ones who suffer most from violence on television. Males are usually the aggressors. In addition, males also tend to be shown as more rational, more stable, and smarter.

Minority and foreign women are the most frequent

prey of the aggressors. For every ten perpetrators of violence, twenty-two minority women and twenty-one foreign women are the targets of violence.[22]

DEFENDERS OF
VIOLENCE ON TELEVISION

Those who defend violence on television have one main argument. They say that the evidence proving that television influences violent behavior is not conclusive. The many research studies that are available do not definitively support the theory that viewing violence on television causes an increase in subsequent aggression in the real world.

Jib Fowles, a professor of human sciences at the University of Houston, believes that many scientists jump to conclusions about television viewing and aggression. He agrees with the Eron data, for example, which show a high correlation between frequency of television viewing, especially of violent shows, and aggressive behavior. But he disagrees with the conclusions of this study. "A correlation does not a cause make," as he put it.

Fowles finds more of a connection between a harsh family life and subsequent aggression than between television violence and aggression. Children growing up in pressurized and punitive households, he believes, will turn to television violence to work off the anger that they cannot discharge at the adults in their lives. Since television may ease the burden but not remove it entirely, they'll still be hostile in later life.[23]

Professor Paul M. Hirsch of the Graduate School of Business at the University of Chicago challenges Dr. Gerbner's research. He questions the relationship Gerbner finds between heavy television viewing and feelings of fear and anxiety. If the relationship does exist, Professor Hirsch thinks, then extreme viewers (over eight hours a day) should be more fearful than heavy viewers (four to eight), but they aren't. Extreme viewers are generally less apprehensive than heavy viewers. Continuing this line of thinking, Professor Hirsch asks: Shouldn't non-viewers be the least fearful of all? Yet, Hirsch discovered, nonviewers were among the most frightened. Thus, he found no relationship between the time spent watching television and the degree of fearfulness.[24]

As for the side-by-side rise in crime rates with the increase of television viewing, Professor Fowles believes that there is no connection. The zooming crime rate, he believes, is not due to television but to the baby-boom generation of children. "Statistically speaking, crime is the handiwork of the young. . . . The sheer numbers of this particular group was enough to make the general crime rates take off."

Far from agreeing that the mayhem on television is destructive, a few researchers see it as allowing for the healthful discharge of viewers' pent-up aggressions. They point out that human violence predates television violence. Violence, they say, has always been part of life, and its appearance in art dates back at least to ancient Greece.

Dr. Seymour Feshback, head of the psychology department at the University of California at Los Angeles, conducted an important experimental field study in 1971 on the effects of television violence on semidelinquent youths. Feshback divided 625 boys, ages nine to fifteen, who lived in special residences, into two groups. For six weeks, the first group watched only boisterous adventure shows. The other group watched only what were considered neutral shows.

At the end of the project, Dr. Feshback found that there was a tendency for the viewers of the action-packed programs to be far less aggressive than the boys exposed to the neutral shows. Those who watched the action-adventure shows actually proved to be less rowdy.

Writes Professor Fowles: "Television violence can decrease hostile feelings by means of the psychological mechanism known to the ancient Greeks—catharsis, the purging of repressed emotions by watching dramas. Members identify with certain characteristics and vicariously act out harbored emotions like fear and anger."[25] Law-enforcement television programs, for example, give viewers an opportunity to discharge some of their own aggressions, since forcefulness used in the name of the law is approved and sanctioned by society.

Sports telecasts also provide a harmless discharge of hostility, some say. The fans identify with the home team and look on the opposing team as the enemy. It is the same as the good guys against the bad guys in action-adventure shows. Millions find in sports broadcasts the perfect antidote to the tensions and resentments of their daily lives. In the fall of 1987, when pro football was off the airwaves because of a players' strike, some families actually experienced more squabbling and antagonism.

Japanese television airs many American action-adventure series, as well as their own detective shows and samurai-warrior tales, which are chock-full of slaughter and gore. Yet, the Japanese today are among the least violent of all people. Crime has been on the decline there for the past thirty years. The number of homicides is minuscule, and juvenile delinquency is virtually non-existent. Some social scientists conclude that the violence on Japanese television has played a part in releasing aggressive feelings and maintaining social tranquility.

A study by the University of Chicago revealed that people find television, including television with a violent content, restful. The subjects reported feeling more relaxed after watching a violent film on television than before. A social scientist at the University of Chicago outfitted 104 adults with beepers and had them paged at random intervals during the course of a week to find out what they were doing and what their mood was. The most notable among his findings, he reported, was that TV watching is experienced as the most relaxing of all activities.

Defenders of television violence also claim that a host of other factors may contribute to real-life violence. Therefore, they say, it is virtually impossible to isolate the effect of television and extremely difficult to come up with conclusive results. They insist that the idea that crime can be cut by banishing violence on television is a delusion.

Amidst all the attempts to disavow the harmful effects of violent television is one simple possibility. The public outcry may be due to the newness of the medium. As the newest mass medium, television serves as a "whipping boy," much like penny newspapers, dime novels, movies, and radio have been in their turn. With time, some expect, attention will shift to newer media, and the studies on television's effects will seem out of date.

IV—7 RECOMMENDATIONS

Television violence may be only one of many causes of real-life violence. Exactly how much it contributes to violent acts in society will probably never be known for sure, since violent behavior depends on such a wide variety of factors. Yet, there are those who feel that television violence is one of the causes of violence over which society can have some control.

Broadcasters, however, have no legal obligation to work to control or lower the increasing aggressiveness on television. But all broadcasters, under regulations of the Federal Communications Commission, do have a legal obligation to deliver programs that serve "the public interest, convenience, and necessity."

George Comstock, writing on juvenile crime, offers some suggestions for the portrayal of violence on television:

1. Criminal and violent acts should not be rewarded by social approval, sexual conquest, or material gain; if possible, they should be punished.

2. Bitter and ruthless conflicts between persons and groups should not be portrayed as the ordinary state of affairs.

3. Mass murders and the elimination of large groups of people should not be portrayed in a way that suggests human life is of little value.

4. Tightly knit, loyal groups should not be depicted as splitting apart in a way that indicates that bonds promise little human security.

5. Extreme and excessive violence should be avoided because it risks inciting violence as well as leaving viewers unresponsive and desensitized.

6. Violence should not be "sanitized" and should be shown to have painful and sometimes horrifying consequences for the victim and for those around him or her.

7. Characters that commit violent acts and crime should not always appear young and good-looking.

8. Violent portrayals on television should not create the impression that violence is appropriate in certain situations.

9. Violent acts should not be portrayed in circumstances ordinarily considered peaceful, such as a classroom or a neighborhood grocery, because it may make the acts seem more plausible.

10. In fictional drama, it should be clear that the violent events are part of a story, not an accurate account of real events, because fact is more likely to be taken as a model for behavior than fiction.[26]

Industry representatives, including the National Association of Broadcasters, have also set standards for the portrayal of violence.

Among their recommendations are:

1. The industry should undertake longitudinal research to develop greater understanding of the relationships between televised and film violence and real-world violence.

2. Movie and television producers and marketers should be required to pay for and carry out research detailing the potential harmful and beneficial effects of each new television series and commercial movie that contains violence.

3. Finally, parents, teachers, and young people should be educated on the possible harmful effects of television and film violence. Then, they can voluntarily restrict their own viewing of televised violence or pressure the television and film industry to offer more nonviolent, prosocial fare.

CHAPTER

VIOLENCE AND
THE MOVIES

- *In* Psycho, *an attractive young woman stays for the night in a motel, where she is savagely stabbed to death in the shower by a complete stranger—all without any apparent motive.*

- *A knife-wielding psychotic threatens the campers and staff of a summer camp in* Friday the 13th; *during a fight for her life, the heroine decapitates the killer.*

- Cop *(1988) tells the story of a serial killer who specializes in the gruesome murders of young women.*

- Colors *(1988), which deals with Los Angeles street gangs, uses actual members of the Crips and Bloods as extras.*

- *The rap film* Tougher Than Leather *(1988) features rappers who slug a police officer after they have decided to take the law into their own hands.*

Movies, some say, cannot have the same freedom as the other arts. Movies are a mass medium, whereas literature, theater, painting, and so on, are directed at small audiences. This reasoning has been used to justify the censorship of movies. The original Motion Picture Production Code explained it this way: "Most arts appeal to the mature. This art [movies] appeals at once to *every class*, mature, immature, developed, undeveloped, law-abiding, criminal. . . . Psychologically, the larger the audience, the lower the moral mass resistance to suggestion."[1]

Some still accept this argument. But many others oppose any censorship of the movies. They say that filmmakers should have the same freedom of expression as any other creative artists because film is no different from any of the other arts and must be protected by our constitutional safeguards.

THE HISTORY OF MOVIE CENSORSHIP

From 1908 and the days of the silent films through 1922, there were no checks placed on those who would depict violence in the movies. Films mirrored the violence and crime in America's big cities.

Nevertheless, a number of individuals attempted to censor what was shown on the screen. Mostly, they based their responses on one main assumption. Film portrayals of crime and violence might encourage similar behavior on the part of young viewers. For a long time, their actions were upheld by the Supreme Court.

The first such ruling came in 1915, in the case of *Mutual Film Corporation* v. *Industrial Commission of Ohio*. The Court said that movies were "a business pure and simple" and therefore not entitled to the same protection under the First Amendment as the printed media.

However, the censors had very little real influence on the content of movies until the 1920s. The trigger for reform came during the "Roaring Twenties," a time that glamorized crime, drinking, and sex and showed a general contempt for the law. Gangster movies that mixed romance with violence were especially popular.

The outcry to censor the movies came from a real-life

incident, not a particular movie. A young actress, Virginia Rappe, died under mysterious circumstances at a party hosted by film star Roscoe (Fatty) Arbuckle. Even though Arbuckle insisted that he was innocent and was three times acquitted of the crime, he became the scapegoat for all that was evil and dangerous in Hollywood. The outraged public perceived the movies as having a bad influence on the lives of people they touched.

In 1921, the movie industry formed an organization called the Motion Picture Producers and Distributors Association of America (MPPDAA). The purpose was to establish some controls over the content of the movies. Will Hays, postmaster general under President Warren G. Harding and an extremely religious man, was appointed head of the group.

For a while, the public seemed satisfied. But by 1930, perhaps due to the Depression and reduced business, the movies introduced even more violence as a way of attracting audiences. The film studios played down the romance and love interest and focused more on criminal activities. Gangsters became attractive heroes and themes often dealt with how they fought off rival mobs.

A rash of gangster movies made between 1930 and 1934, starring either James Cagney or Edward G. Robinson, set off another flood of protests against so-called degeneracy in the movies. A campaign got under way to boycott movies that were deemed offensive. This provided Hays with the support he needed to enforce the Motion Picture Production Code.

In 1934 Hollywood started regulating crime films according to the code's pronouncements. In the area of violence, for example, there were some specific prohibitions: Theft, robbery, safecracking, and dynamiting of trains, mines, buildings, etc., were not to be described in detail. There were to be no scenes showing law-enforcement officers such as private detectives or bank guards "dying at the hands of criminals."

Under pressure from such groups as the Roman Catholic Legion of Decency and the Federal Council of Churches, the industry promised to deny distribution to any films that did not receive the code's "Seal of Approval." Most film producers and studio executives felt they had no choice but to avoid a "Condemned" rating. Certain others came up with ways to feature violence but to get around the censorship rules.

One scheme featured fast-paced, violent action but sidestepped the code by making the lawmen the violent ones. In his films made between 1935 and 1939, for example, James Cagney switched sides and used his guns and fists to uphold justice. Stephen Farber, in his book *The Movie Rating Game*, quotes a film historian who says, "In gangster movies it was simply a question of getting more law and order, as a counterbalance, into a picture which was pretty well devoted to violent crime."

This formula for making films was soon exhausted, and by 1939 Hollywood had to find another way to put violence on the screen. During the early 1940s, crimes in the movies became even more brutal. For example, the film *This Gun for Hire* (1942) created a model for a psychopathic killer. Its star, Alan Ladd, plays a gunman who has no sense of right and wrong, is vicious, cold-blooded, and extremely clever. The characters in early-forties films, in general, grew more cruel and dishonest. And to justify the increased violence, the heroes were often portrayed as patriots fighting foreign soldiers or spies.

Toward the end of the decade, filmmakers revived their interest in screen gangsters. *The Killers* (1946), *Brute Force* (1947), *Kiss of Death* (1947), and *White Heat* (1949) exploited gangland violence, menacing killers, rival hoodlums, and spectacular action scenes.

Nevertheless, the prospect of censorship hung over the heads of American filmmakers. Writers and producers were forced to modify or eliminate any story points that the code office considered harmful.

CHALLENGES
TO CENSORSHIP

The first challenges to the Motion Picture Production Code came in some decisions handed down by the U.S. Supreme Court in 1948. By then, an estimated 95 percent of all films shown in the United States bore the code's Seal of Approval.[2] In *United States* v. *Paramount Pictures* (1948), the Court made an important ruling. Major motion-picture companies could no longer control giant theater chains.

Independently produced movies, without the code seal, could now get into the theaters more easily. In the *Paramount* decision, Justice William O. Douglas questioned the legal basis of film censorship for the first time. He wrote: "We have no doubt that motion pictures, like newspapers and radio, are included in the press whose freedom is guaranteed by the First Amendment."[3]

Four years later, this right of freedom of expression for the movies was even more firmly established. The Supreme Court's decision in *Burstyn* v. *Wilson* (1952) ruled against most local censorship boards. The Court found that the ban against the Italian film *The Miracle* on the grounds that it was sacrilegious, was unconstitutional. This established the principle that expression by means of motion pictures is included within the free speech protection of the Constitution.

The advent of television, in the decade from 1950 to 1959, presented a major challenge to Hollywood. The industry had to find a way to draw fans away from the novelty of home TV sets and bring them back into the movie houses. The solution involved putting an end to the old image of screen gangsters and introducing new, even more violent heroes. Among some typical examples are the following: the sadistic thug in *The Big Heat* (1953); the violent prisoner in *Riot in Cell Block 11* (1954); the detective more brutal than the criminals he pursues in *Kiss Me Deadly* (1955); and the old-time hood in *Al Capone* (1959).

Because of its increasing competition with television, the film industry struck back in the 1960s with a series of blockbuster films. They were in step with the revolutionary new attitudes on sexual freedom, drugs, civil rights, student protests, and acceptable levels of violence. Three movies, especially, brought a fresh outcry for film censorship: *Bonnie and Clyde* (1967), for its daring, reckless, senseless crimes; *Point Blank* (1967), for its vengeful killer; and *Madigan* (1968), for its police brutality.

FROM CENSORSHIP
TO CLASSIFICATION

Even though the courts ruled that motion pictures were protected under the First Amendment, there was still considerable concern as to the effect of some movies on young people. One Supreme Court decision, *Ginsberg* v. *New York* (1968), established a legal distinction between the rights of adults and those of children. It ruled that material constitutionally protected for adults could still be considered objectionable for minors.

Another case, *Interstate Circuit* v. *Dallas* (1968), struck down the classification system used by the city of Dallas but indicated that more carefully drawn standards *could* survive a constitutional test. The decision cleared the way for state and municipal classification. It also made the industry recognize that it would have to establish its own rating system if it wanted to prevent an outbreak of local rating boards such as existed during the 1920s.

Between June and September of 1968, the Motion Picture Association of America (MPAA) worked out the details for a rating system that defined a film's suitability for children. The plan, which went into effect on November 1, assigned one of four ratings to all films:

G: All ages admitted; general audiences.

M: (Now PG) Parental guidance suggested; some material may not be suitable for children.

R: Restricted; anyone under sixteen (now seventeen) requires an accompanying parent or adult.

X: No one under sixteen (now eighteen or twenty-one, depending on the state) admitted.

As of July 1, 1984, another rating was added.

PG-13: Parents are strongly cautioned to give specific guidance for attendance of children under thirteen; some material may be inappropriate for young children.

Classification of movies, in theory at least, is not the work of a censor. A censor is defined as someone who removes or prohibits any material he or she considers unsuitable. The MPAA's Code and Rating Administration does not remove or prohibit anything. What it purports to do is to define a film's suitability for young people.[4]

Still, some wonder whether the rating board should have the power to bar teenagers from X-rated movies. By restricting attendance at certain films, the rating board is in effect also restricting free access to ideas and information.

For adults, the problem may be even more disturbing. In practice, the distinction between censorship and classification tends to blur. Even though the rating board does no more than simply label films, this causes filmmakers to change the content of their pictures—at all stages of production—just to be sure to get the rating they want. Some films are never even produced, distributed, or exhibited because they are threatened with an X rating. Strictly speaking, the rating board cannot ban a film, but the rating given often has the same effect. It limits what filmmakers feel they can produce and what audiences feel they can see.

Many people use the ratings to help them select movies. But few are completely satisfied with the present system. Some moviegoers feel that the ratings are too lenient; others that they are too severe. Some consider them overly sensitive to sex as opposed to violence; others say they are so inconsistent as to be virtually meaningless.

A number of experts call the years from 1970 to 1978 an "almost-anything-goes" time in the movies. The most successful and profitable films featured murders, beatings, brawls, rapes, and other forms of violence. The films stressed sensationalism and ignored story line and human relationships. Some believe they captured the vulgarity, greed, deceit, and cruelty of American life. Two examples of this trend are *The French Connection* (1971), which showed police brutality, and *Chinatown* (1974), with its excessive violence.

Stanley Kubrick's film *A Clockwork Orange* (1971) set off a whole new round of complaints about excessive violence in the movies. The famous rape scene in that film lasts a full ten minutes, which is a very long time in a motion picture. Some people classify *A Clockwork Orange* with other so-called violation movies. This group includes *The Desperate Hours* (1955), *Wait Until Dark* (1967), and *In Cold Blood* (1967). The common thread through them all is a real or threatened attack on innocent, decent people by violent and frequently obsessed men.

THE IMPACT
OF FILM VIOLENCE
One of the first kinds of motion picture to tell the story and reveal character by means of a fast-moving plot and vigorous action was the western. Basically, the plots put the main character, a male, in dangerous situations where courage and honor come before anything else in his life. The hero strikes out for what he wants—be it land, cattle, water, or gold—but is resisted by equally strong men.

Inasmuch as the characters represent moral values, the plot of a western usually ends in some kind of duel to the death and an end to evil. Because of the constant threat of violence and the nearness of death, guns are at the center of these dramas. The pistol is always at the ready. It's only a matter of time before the gun battle erupts, usually leading to the violent death of the villain.

Take *Butch Cassidy and the Sundance Kid* (1969) as an example. Two robbers, hounded by lawmen, flee from America to Bolivia, where they are hunted down and trapped by hundreds of soldiers. Faced with the choice of surrender or death, they choose to come out with guns roaring and die defiantly. In Sam Peckinpah's *The Wild Bunch*, released the same year, violence flares on all sides, and the gang's leaders also die in a final gun battle.

Although the western appeals mostly to males, this kind of film is a great audience-pleaser. The genre generally succeeds because it depicts people who are personally free, clear-thinking on issues, and certain of their purpose in life. The western is a far cry from the troubles of contemporary life. The western hero never suffers from being dominated or humiliated by a boss or being confused by conflicting moral standards.

When watching westerns, then, the viewers get a vicarious feeling of being in charge of their lives and their destiny. Unfortunately, the westerns also emphasize the worst aspects of frontier mentality—toleration of violence, disregard for human lives, and admiration for lawbreakers who willingly use their guns to get what they want.

The criminologists Gresham Sykes and Thomas Drabek have written, "We seem to remember our sheriffs and our outlaws with equal pleasure."[5] For some reason, as Sykes and Drabek point out, Hollywood has made over twenty movies about Billy the Kid. In real life, Billy was described as a short youth "who looks like a cretin." But in the movies, Billy was played by such handsome, romantic heroes as Paul Newman and Kris Kristofferson.

Like the western, the war film emphasizes bravery— the courage to fight. War films tend to legitimize violence and give the hero the job of executing it. The war film is similar to the western in that the concept of honor pervades the action. Quarrels and hostilities arise inevitably as men from different walks of life prepare to face battle together. Some war films portray the confusion and pain of battle amid scenes of overpowering violence and brutality. As Roy Paul Madsen wrote in the 1970s, "In the contemporary war film, the viewer is less likely to see waving flags than oozing entrails."

Male viewers tend to identify with the sight of brave men fighting—even when the consequences are horrible. War films owe their popularity to the fact that they provide a sense of adventure, comradeship, escapism, and easy solutions to life's difficult problems. The films trick the viewer into accepting a double standard of morality: an attack is good if carried out by our side and evil if carried out by the other side.

Laboratory studies on the effects of film violence on aggression show that hostility toward an enemy is likely to be increased if the subject sees a film portraying a victim similar to the enemy.[6] Public hostility toward minority groups, for example, can be increased by films that portray "justified" violence against such groups.

The gangster film is as American an art form as the western. But the usual concept of good guys and bad guys is reversed. Neither the gangster nor the police show very much concern with morality. The gangster is usually a loner thumbing his nose at the world and backing up his defiance with a machine gun. And the police are often prepared to use any means, including excessive violence, to capture the criminal and bring him or her to justice.

Gangster-film plots are often based on the newspaper headlines of the 1930s. The essential theme is, grab the money and run and kill whoever tries to stop you. In the course of the action, the gangster character shoots men in the back, beats women, and breaks the arms and legs of those who get in his way. The stories are filled with armed combat between rival hoodlums and between them and the police. The gangster almost always shoots first, often for the most trivial reason, and is traditionally shown as unstable and unpredictable.

Lincoln Kirstein, writing in *Hound & Horn* (1932), said that the concept of the American hero had changed from the "lean, shrewd, lantern-jawed, slow-voiced, rangy, blond American pioneer" to "a short, red-headed Irishman, quick to wrath, humorous, articulate in anger, representing not a minority in action, but the action of the American majority—the semi-literate lower middle class."[7] Kirstein went on to say this about James Cagney: "No one expresses more clearly in terms of pictorial action the delights of violence, the overtones of semi-conscious sadism, the tendency towards destruction, towards anarchy which is the basis of American sex-appeal."[8]

Although once the gangster film was based on daily headlines, today the concept has changed. In recent times, the hero is more likely to be an unscrupulous businessman who resorts on occasion to the gun as an effective way to do business.

Some see the early gangster films as providing an emotional release—a kind of cultural catharsis. The gangster who ignores the law and mores of a society (which were being questioned anyway) was making a social comment. Even respectable people could sympathize with tough guys who were born good but went bad in a system loaded with injustice.

The gun-toting gangster has become a folk hero for a couple of reasons. His battles against authority are applauded by all those who are angry at society and its institutions. And he provides vicarious excitement and relief, as well as wish fulfillment, for those who secretly wish to gun down a driver who cuts them off or to blow up a bank vault and steal all the money.

Apropos of vicarious thrills, actor Lee Marvin made the following remarks about his film *The Killers:*

*In the opening, me and my partner sidle into a blind
home looking for a doublecross. I get behind the head
blind dame, grab her by the throat and push her almost
to the floor. "Where's Johnny North?" I breathe in her
ear. So she tells us. I barge into the room knocking the
blindees over—we used real ones—and I say "You
Johnny North?" He says yeah. So we take out our guns
and we put ten bullets in him straight up and down
his middle. It's great. And everybody out front is getting their vicarious thrills.*[9]

Film writer Robert Warshow suggests that gangster films
deal more with the modern, urban experience than with
the problem of crime in American life. In his opinion, the
gangster expresses that part of the American psyche that
rejects the qualities and demands of modern life, which
rejects "Americanism" itself.

Most of the early classic gangster films end with the
death of the gangster-hero. This was to conform to the
official dictates of the motion picture industry creed that
insisted that the guilty criminal must be punished. There
was very little in these films that was not essential to the
development of the plot or to showing the protagonists'
lowly character. Few, if any, killings were shown on the
screen. And the fact that the bad guys were always punished was intentional. It showed that crime did not pay.

Over the decades, the approach and the concept of
honor changed in the gangster film. Take *Bonnie and Clyde*,
which dates from 1967. The film shows two criminals
progressing from thrill-seeking acts to vicious, violent
crimes. Its detailed, graphic depiction of killing established a new standard in the portrayal of violence. According to director Arthur Penn's philosophy, "In film,
when you show a death it should have that shock effect.
The trouble with violence in most films is that it is not
violent enough."

Many consider *The Godfather* (1972) "violent enough."
The film has as the gangster an unscrupulous business-

man who uses violence and guns to help him succeed in business. As author Arthur Asa Berger says in his book on film: "A murder is only 'business' to the Mafia (and only Sicilian business at that)."[10]

According to Berger, *The Godfather* was a significant film because it raised an important point about the American character in the 1970s. Had large groups of people in our society given up all belief in the possibilities of legal justice? Had they decided to let might prevail over right?

Some films take an especially "soft" view of the whole concept of violence. Given this outlook, violence depicted in the right way can seem positively beneficial. John Fraser writes this about violence in films: "Compelling men to see themselves as they are, it causes the mask to fall, reveals the lies, the slackness, baseness and hypocrisy of our world."

Of course, this attempt to portray violence as a means of self-expression or self-affirmation can have its own dangers. It may lead to more and more realistically depicted violence. Filmmakers who choose to create the impression that violence can be good will make movies that show violence achieving desired goals.

The spy film, another popular type of motion picture, was born after World War II and is closely identified with the extraordinary fictional Englishman James Bond. Secret-agent Bond has an incredible arsenal of weapons at his disposal—a pistol with a foot-long silencer, backup guns in his tie clip and shoelaces, knockout gas in his cigarette lighter, and so on. Brutal killings and widespread destruction rage through the Bond pictures, even though the violence may be treated in a rather light, campy sort of way.

The genre of motion picture known as the psychodrama has several common characteristics. It usually has a central figure that is alone and vulnerable. The setting is usually ominous and forbidding. The plot devices are carefully chosen to create a terrifying feeling of suspense.

This includes elaborate preparations by the villain for an act of violence, repeated postponement of the inevitable violent climax, and the betrayal or sudden transformation of a trusted friend into an unexpected enemy. Death, or the threat of death, is an integral part of the film.

In the psychodrama, scenes depicting suicide or extreme violence are an important part of the action. Kidnapping and sadism are put in to heighten the shock value and audience appeal. In all three *Omen* films (starting in 1976), for instance, unbelievably freakish "accidents" keep happening. In *The Omen*, a man has his head cut off by a flying sheet of glass; in *Damien-Omen II*, a doctor's body is split in two in an elevator murder.

The extreme type of psychodrama is the horror film. Horror films are often gruesome and usually border on the sexually violent, or pornographic. The characters include monsters from other planets who are so powerful that no bullet can stop them, demented scientists with superhuman abilities, wild beasts trained to attack and kill humans, bloodsucking vampires, and, of course, innocent victims quaking with fear. Most horror films present so much blood, gore, and violence that after a while the viewer loses the ability to be frightened, revolted, or shocked.

The proliferation of horror films in the 1950s showed a preoccupation with depriving people of human or individual qualities. Even a film that gives an illusion of normalcy, as in *Invasion of the Body Snatchers* (1956), hides a deep-rooted violence.

George A. Romero's *Night of the Living Dead* (1968) was among the first films to be based on a horror comic book. It tells of a group of people who hide in an abandoned farmhouse and are terrorized by some gruesome flesh-eating zombies. The success of this picture paved the way for a number of increasingly frightening and grisly films that followed.

Recently, the partnership of Frank Henenlotter and Edgar Ievins produced several cheaply made horror-thrillers. Among them are *Basket Case* (1982) and *Brain Damage* (1988). The star of *Brain Damage* is a skull-sucking eel-like creature that slips its needlelike tongue into a young man's brain, injecting a blue fluid that gives the youth a druglike high. The youth becomes hooked on the monster and is soon finding suitable victims for him to prey on. These mass-distribution movies have been widely shown.

THE CONTROVERSY

In the forefront of those who publicly discuss the dangers of graphic violence on the screen are the film-critic team of Gene Siskel and Roger Ebert. When Paramount Pictures released *Friday the 13th*, both critics wrote that the film was excessively violent and extremely vicious in its attitude toward women. A series of similar films followed—*He Knows You're Alone* (1980), *Silent Scream* (1980), *The Boogey Man* (1980), and *Fade to Black* (1980).

The men first called for a boycott of Paramount films. Then, they launched a bitter attack on what they termed "a disturbing new trend in today's movies." These movies, they argued, direct most of their violence at women who are independent types. The underlying message seems to be that strong women must somehow be punished. Characteristically, the women get their "comeuppance" at the hands of killers who transform them into screaming victims.

Author John McCarty argues that "splatter" movies—those in which everything and everyone is splashed with blood—grew out of forty years of film censorship and restriction. He says that they are not antiwomen or anti–anything else, for that matter. "If Siskel and Ebert really want to run splatter movies out of town," McCarty says, "all they need do is bite their tongues, sit back, and wait a bit, for splatter cinema will eventually run its course and fade away."[11]

But the main fear that most critics have about violent movies is that they make the audience seek *real* violence.

This argument is based on the assumption that people go to see violent films because they genuinely enjoy seeing them. Film-violence opponents suggest that the thrill viewers get from the fights and battles and the pain and suffering on the screen makes them want to keep the sensation going after they leave the theater.

A National Institute of Justice publication refers to a study of fifty-eight incidents of alleged movie-inspired violence. A number of incidents involved imitation of the famous Russian roulette scenes in *The Deer Hunter*. The study, however, concluded that "no clear evidence of causal links could be found."[12]

On the other hand, there was a sensational case some years ago in which a fourteen-year-old Columbus, Ohio, youngster accidentally killed his brother with a gun as the two boys played out a scene from the movie *Dirty Harry* (1971). And Dr. Alvin Poussaint has described the impact of *Super Fly*, a movie that glamorized cocaine. Black youngsters in Brooklyn, New York, drastically increased their use of the drug and practically the entire student body of a Los Angeles high school started wearing gold cocaine-spoon necklaces after the West Coast debut of the film.[13]

During the civil-rights movement and the rise of television viewing in the 1960s, young people and blacks came to represent increasingly large portions of the movie audience. In response, there was a rash of so-called "blaxploitation" movies—films in praise of black violence—designed especially to appeal to their interests. One of the frequently encountered scenes in these films is the mass murder, an orgiastic massacre that results in a large number of casualties, mostly white. The blacks who are responsible for all the killing are portrayed as cool and detached and show little compassion, emotion, or interest.

Commander Joe DiLeonardi is head of the Chicago Police Homicide Section, a department that investigated a series of unrelated murders and robbery-murders. Di-

Leonardi says that the methods and language used by the slayers were exact imitations of recent blaxploitation films. In a number of killings, the murderer announced himself by snarling, "Nigger Charlie is here," repeating the words he had heard on the screen.

Many believe, though, that the escalation of violence in movies is a result, not a cause, of violence in society. The rise, they say, indicates a growing appetite for violence spreading throughout towns and cities across the land. They also argue that the graphic, overdrawn, and sometimes fantastic images of brutality in modern films desensitizes audiences to the threat of real violence in a positive way. It helps people learn to control their fears that violence—rape, murder, robbery, terrorist attack, even the possibility of nuclear war—may someday reach out and claim them as victims, also.

The writer John McCarty echoes this point. He reports that after the atomic bombing of Hiroshima and Nagasaki that ended World War II, Japanese people flocked to see films that portrayed the mass destruction of Japanese cities by grotesque, nuclear-spawned monsters. "Could it be that these 'gore and destruction' movies were being used . . . to transform remembered images of real violence and destruction into images of pure fantasy— thus taking the sting out of them?" If so, it is just as possible that today's audiences are using horror movies to counteract nightly newscasts that bring images of real and escalating violence into our homes every evening.

What of the future of violence in the movies? Will it dwindle naturally, as some critics suggest? Will censors once again toughen restrictions on graphic violence and sex, sending such films underground?

Everyone agrees that there has been a steady and considerable increase in both the bloodiness and explicitness of violence in films over recent decades. Since the new rating system was initiated in 1968, a smaller proportion of films produced and released have been rated

G (suitable for general audiences) and a higher proportion have been rated R (restricted).

In the past, men were traditionally the violent ones, and men and women were the victims. Now, more and more women are shown using guns and knives to establish themselves as full partners in crime—just as capable of violence and aggression as the men.

One factor in the escalating violence of movies is their apparent attempt to compete with television. The movie producers seek to exploit areas of content that were barred from television. "Hollywood mined sectors of the market that television could not reach," Arthur Asa Berger writes. Similarly, the subject matter and the portrayals of human relationships are moving further and further from the restrictions imposed by the old Hays office. Crime and criminals are routinely glorified and frequently escape punishment. Explicit sex and rape have become popular motifs. And all the illusional skills of the film industry are applied to create startlingly realistic scenes of sadistic brutality and mutilation.

Film producers are forever on the lookout for new and more extreme forms of violence. To quote the head of the film company that made *Death Race 2000* (1975), about a cross-country car race that gives points for every pedestrian run over, "Violence is going to escalate because the public always demands more than they saw last time out."

As long as audiences come to the movie theaters to be shocked, scared, and revolted, violent movies will prosper. Following H. L. Mencken's dictum that "You must give a good show to get a crowd, and a good show is one with slaughter in it," most modern critics agree that violence in movies probably will be with us for a long, long time to come.

CHAPTER

CABLE TV AND
DIAL-A-PORN

■ *Teens who stay up past 8 P.M. can watch R-rated films on pay cable.*

■ *At midnight, the children in one metropolitan area can watch a cable program conducted by a performer dressed in a G-string who considers herself an X-rated celebrity.*

■ *A woman said that her young daughter was sexually molested by two brothers after they had listened to a dial-a-porn message on the telephone.[1]*

■ *A twelve-year-old boy spent two and a half hours listening to sexually explicit messages on telephone pornography services. Two weeks later, he sexually assaulted a four-year-old girl.[2]*

The *New York Times* movie critic Vincent Canby was recently flipping through the channels at 8 P.M. on a weekday evening and stumbled onto *Showtime,* a pay-cable station. The channel was showing the horror movie *Friday the 13th: Part IV: The Final Chapter,* which Canby had already seen in a movie theater.

When this film came out in 1984, it carried an R rating (children under seventeen not allowed unless accompanied by an adult). Although moviegoers in the theater might have laughed at the simulated violence and slaughter, Canby found it not the least bit funny when viewed in his own home.

Canby says:

> *Seen at home in the shank of the evening (when thousands of kids are doing their homework, alone in their rooms, with the telly on), the movie took on an entirely different character for me and, I assume, a lot of other people, including the far-under-17 kids who in most circumstances were seeing the film for the first time. . . . The murder of the fat girl that occurs was no longer a joke. It was a wanton, inexplicable vicious act. . . .*[3]

Many people agree with Canby that movies look quite different when they are seen privately. The ratings become meaningless because our responses depend, to some extent, on when and where the movies are seen.

Also, Canby cites a recent issue of *Cable Guide*, received by Manhattan subscribers, that carried the following cheery advertisement: "The dinner dishes are done, the kids are in bed, the worries of the world are behind you for the night. It's time to relax and unwind with some of Hollywood's finest movies. . . ." As Canby points out, these words do not accurately describe the horror and violence in the movies that are so often shown on pay-cable.

Cable television poses a number of unique problems as compared to the other media. Legal experts and citizen groups are now actively engaged in the struggle over attempts to regulate this industry as well as the dial-a-porn system of phone messages.

CABLE TELEVISION

Cable television first appeared in the United States in the 1940s and has been slowly spreading throughout the land since then. The system was first designed to serve subscribers who lived in places where broadcast television signals could not be received. Within a few years, the concept spread to metropolitan centers. As of May 2, 1986, about 60 million of the 85 million television households in the country were connected to cable television.[4]

Cable companies distribute the television shows to subscribers through a closed-circuit wire system. The cable wire is strung along utility poles or buried in an underground conduit and enters the subscriber's home much like a telephone line. This is different from broadcast television, which transmits its signals through the airwaves to anyone in the vicinity with a television set.

Cable television, which includes satellite television, differs from broadcast television in another way. Broadcast television, you may recall, is regulated by the rules and practices of the Federal Communications Commission (FCC). Under current law, cable is not subject to the same regulations. Instead, the system is controlled by the Cable Communications Policy Act of 1984 (CCPA) and is subject to federal, state, and local rules.

Individual local cable operators decide what programs will be offered on their systems. Most cable systems present a basic package of local broadcast channels and at least one of the "pay television" channels, such as Home Box Office (HBO), Cinemax, Showtime, or the Disney Channel. These channels usually carry unedited movies without commercial interruption. The subscriber pays a monthly fee for the basic service and an additional fee for the "pay" television.

The giant publisher Time-Life, Inc., is the country's major owner of cable systems. It owns HBO and Cinemax, the largest pay-cable movie channels, as well as

Channel J in Manhattan, a very explicit porno channel. Time-Life also owns Orion Films and HBO Video, both producers of movie films and television shows. Through these outlets, Time-Life has become one of the leading distributors of slasher/rape-type movies.[5]

In an issue of *Time* magazine, film critic Richard Corliss defends sadomasochism and mourns the "violence done to movies." Basically, Corliss takes the position that the movies are not brutal, violent, or sexually explicit enough. But the National Coalition on Television Violence points out that he writes all this without any mention of Time-Life's stake in the industry!

Charles F. Dolan was a founder in 1961 of Cablevision, one of the country's first television cable systems. He thinks that cable channels will become far more numerous in the near future—"to the point of infinity."[6] Cable will soon make available a more complete range of entertainment and information. When asked whether Cablevision is, among other things, a seller of pornography, Dolan responded that it was not a matter for Cablevision to decide. The decision of what programs were seen was up to the viewers at home.

In Dolan's opinion, it is hard to stumble across X-programming. It is on a particular channel, and as it is on a pay channel it cannot reach a home unless specifically ordered. He considers the cable companies more reluctant than the corner video store or the neighborhood magazine stand to make X-rated material available. Video stores and magazines offer content that could never go on the cable system, he claims.

CABLEPORN

"Cableporn" is a term that some people use to describe material on cable television that they find sexually offensive. As we said, because cablecasting is not transmitted through the airwaves, it is not covered by the broadcasting law, which prohibits the broadcasting of obscene or indecent programs on radio or television. Some people want the same regulation of cable as there is of broadcasting. Different technology or not, they say, it comes into the home through the same television set.

Nevertheless, cablecasting does not currently come under the provisions of the broadcasting law. Only cable television programming judged obscene is presently prohibited by law. Cable TV and satellite transmissions cannot offer obscene programming but have been permitted to show material considered indecent. "Indecent," you will recall, is a word defined by a 1978 Supreme Court decision to describe language or material that may be offensive as measured by contemporary community standards.

A Junior League survey found that roughly forty-eight uncut films rated R by the MPAA appear on pay-cable every year.[7] The movies in the R category received that rating because they depict violence or nudity or contain sexually explicit or profane language.

Recently, many attempts have been made to regulate so-called indecent, nonobscene programming. But some fear that these efforts at regulation could ban from cable television such Academy Award–winning films as *Kramer v. Kramer*, *The Godfather*, and *Coming Home*.

The rock-music cable channel, MTV, makes parents particularly nervous, since many of its offerings are unfamiliar and have not been edited for a general audience. Some cable guides give one- or two-word clues, such as "violent" or "sex explicit." Other than that, parents have little guidance in evaluating the programs their children watch.

Not long ago the Attorney General's Commission on Pornography considered whether or not to recommend changes in the law that would bar material that is "indecent" as well as obscene from cable TV, just as it is from radio and broadcast television. The members were divided in their opinions. Some believed in the rigorous enforcement of obscenity laws, combined with enforcement of "lockbox" requirements, so that parents can prevent their children from seeing such material. Some held that the suggested changes were unconstitutional for cable, and perhaps even for broadcast television. Others urged that changes be made to restrict pure violence, rather than indecency. And the final group felt that the regulation of the legally obscene should be the same for cable as for broadcast television.

Among the suggested solutions to the cableporn problem is the "turn the dial" approach. It holds that viewers who do not want to expose themselves or their children to pornography should simply switch to another channel.

Dissenters insist that the "turn the dial" argument does not hold up. Switching channels to avoid pornography, according to this view, is like running away after being attacked by a mugger. They want a law passed that prohibits cableporn from being transmitted through the cable wires in the first place.[8]

Once cableporn programs are brought into a community, they become part of the community. Signals of cableporn channels sometimes "bleed" over into the sets of people who don't subscribe to them. Even if the video picture is scrambled, the audio signals may come across perfectly clear.

The National Coalition on Television Violence supports the censorship of pornography that is violent and depicts sexual violence, but they have never specifically come out in favor of such legislation. Rather, they believe that the surgeon general's views on violent entertainment should get equal time with statements from the producers of violence.[9]

According to the NCTV, research studies show that strict codes regarding violent films and TV programs increase freedom of speech rather than stifle it. As examples, they cite countries such as Sweden and New

Zealand. The rating systems in these nations are more strict than those in the United States, but there is less political censorship, and more differing points of view are expressed than in this country.

CABLE PROGRAMMING
AND THE FIRST AMENDMENT

Two significant Supreme Court rulings relate to the regulation of cable television in the U.S. They are *Miller* v. *California* (1973) and *FCC* v. *Pacifica Foundation* (1978).

The *Miller* case concerned the mass mailing of unsolicited advertisements regarding so-called adult material. In its ruling, the Court set forth a three-part test for "obscene" speech—speech unprotected by the First Amendment.

The Court held that for speech to be obscene: "the average person, applying contemporary community standards, would find that the work, taken as a whole, appeals to the prurient interest . . . the work depicts or describes in a patently offensive way, sexual conduct specifically defined by the applicable state law, and the work taken as a whole lacks serious literary, artistic, political, or scientific value." [10]

Thus, it is up to the "triers of fact," juries or judges, to decide what is obscene under the guidelines, putting themselves in the place of the average person to determine or apply community standards.

Those opposed to regulation of cable television say that strict compliance is necessary, based on *all* three parts of the test for obscenity. Community standards is not *the* test for obscenity but a *part* of the test for obscenity. The Court's opinion, they say, ensures that "no one will be subject to prosecution for the sale or exposure of obscene materials unless these materials depict or describe patently offensive 'hard core' sexual conduct." [11]

Morality in Media is a national organization devoted to the vigorous enforcement of obscenity laws, particularly at the federal level. The community sets up standards for itself and has a right to legislate to protect those standards, they say.

At issue in the *Pacifica* case was a radio broadcast of a monologue aired at 2 P.M. that was heard by a man driving with his young son. The man was shocked by the material contained in the monologue. He filed a complaint with the FCC, which held that it was permitted under the First Amendment to regulate an "indecent" radio broadcast that was not obscene.

After a number of appeals, the case reached the Supreme Court. The Court concluded that, "the special interest of the federal government in regulation of the broadcast media does not readily translate into justification for regulation of other means of communication." Since the original ruling, several courts have held that "*Pacifica's* rationale is inappropriate in the context of cable television regulation."

After the 1978 *Pacifica* ruling, several state and local attempts were made to regulate indecent, nonobscene cable programming. In each instance, the courts rejected such efforts as restraints of free speech fully protected by the First Amendment. In *Home Box Office* v. *Wilkinson* (1982), the ruling emphasized the importance of the freedom of choice in cable television and an individual's decision to subscribe to cable's varied programming. As Judge Bruce Sterling Jenkins observed: "Within constitutional limits, an individual's choice to indulge in watching cable TV a lot, a little, or choosing not to indulge at all, should be his or her own."[12]

The position of Morality in Media is that it is not up to the viewer to avoid objectionable programs. The obligation rests with the cable operator not to transmit pornography. By transmitting pornography through the wire, the cable operator inflicts pornography on the community, thus breaking the law.

DIAL-A-PORN RECORDINGS

In the 1920s, the Bell Telephone Company began offering recorded messages, called "Dial-it" services, to its customers. At first, Dial-it only gave the time of day and the weather. By the 1970s, though, the service grew to include such recorded messages as jokes, prayers, and sports and racetrack results. In the early 1980s, the FCC ruled that the phone companies could not both provide the recorded messages and transmit the calls.

Soon after, in 1982, the so-called dial-a-porn services began, with outside organizations supplying the messages. There are two types of dial-a-porn calls. In the first type, the customer dials a number and carries on a live conversation with a paid performer who encourages sexual acts and fantasies during the course of the phone conversation. The caller is then billed for an amount usually between $15 and $30.

The customer who dials a number for the second type of call hears a prerecorded message. The acts described on the messages may include sodomy, rape, incest, bestiality, sadomasochistic abuse, and sex acts with children. The caller is charged for each call on the regular monthly telephone bill.

On June 6, 1984, the FCC, which regulates dial-a-porn activities, issued guidelines limiting access to dial-a-porn until after 9 P.M. as a way of controlling children's use of the service. After an appeal by Carlin Communication, though, dial-a-porn became available round-the-clock once again. Then, on October 16, 1985, the FCC came out with new regulations, which require special access codes or the use of credit cards to gain access to the recorded telephone messages. Many dial-a-porn operators, however, have ignored the FCC regulations. In fact, on April 12, 1988, the FCC fined two California dial-a-porn companies $600,000 each for not limiting access to their services.[13]

More than 70 million Dial-it calls were handled by AT&T in the year 1987. The local Dial-it numbers of the New York Telephone Company attracted 405 million calls in the same year, many placed by boys and girls still in elementary school. Most of the messages could be considered sexually explicit and legally obscene. The companies that provided these services earned about $1.2 million from the operation.[14]

The dial-a-porn numbers are openly advertised in pornographic newspapers and magazines and even appear in some telephone directories. Since many of these newspapers and magazines are sold at newsstands and convenience stores, the phone numbers are easily available to youngsters. The Attorney General's Commission finds this very worrisome, especially as dial-a-porn descriptions of unlawful, violent, and incestuous acts are usually used to achieve sexual arousal.

The telephone companies have mixed feelings about dial-a-porn. On the one hand, they find dial-a-porn deplorable. Yet, they support Dial-it services as a means of providing information to the public and earning extra income. And they argue that legally they cannot deny anyone the use of telephone lines.

One day in June 1987, a twelve-year-old boy spent two and a half hours listening to sexually explicit messages on a dial-a-porn line. Two weeks later he sexually assaulted a four-year-old girl. The boy's parents joined with the girl's parents in a lawsuit against the phone company and the providers of the explicit material. The suit argued that the companies' negligence in allowing minors to call for messages caused the incident, making both children victims.

The parents of both children allege that Pacific Bell is motivated by profit. For the year ending June 30, 1987, the company earned $71.7 million from its various Dial-it services. California alone has about 200 dial-a-porn companies, most of which charge $2 a call.[15]

Pornography opponents hope this case will be the "knockout punch" to minors' access to dial-a-porn messages. Others argue that the lawsuit will not succeed. They cite an unsuccessful suit that alleged that a sexual assault of a nine-year-old girl in San Francisco in 1974 was "stimulated" by a similar assault in the movie *Born Innocent*, which was telecast four nights earlier. The case was dismissed in 1978 on First Amendment grounds, and the plaintiffs' lawyer acknowledged that he could not prove that the movie constituted incitement to break the law and thus should not be protected by the First Amendment.

But the plaintiffs in the dial-a-porn case plan to stress the distinctions between television broadcasts and the telephone. They argue that the telephone is not subject to the standards of what is suitable for children that television broadcasts followed. And they will point out that parents cannot monitor children's phone calls as easily as they can control their television viewing.

As in other disputes over pornography, the First Amendment right to freedom of speech is a key issue. Because of constitutional concerns, the Public Utilities Commission does not allow telephone companies to censor the messages or to discriminate among Dial-it services on the basis of content.

At the heart of the issue are two basic questions: Does listening to sexually stimulating messages incite children to sexually violent or criminal behavior? And who determines whether a particular message is sexually stimulating, indecent, or obscene?

A decision in an Arizona case tried by the U.S. Court of Appeals for the Ninth Circuit in San Francisco went a long way to changing the view of what is constitutionally permissible. On September 14, 1987, the court upheld Mountain Bell's decision not to provide service to companies offering pornographic messages. The court said that the policy served the useful purpose for society of protecting its children and thus was not practicing unlawful discrimination. Lawyers for Carlin Communication, Inc., a message provider based in New York City, have petitioned the Appeals Court for a rehearing of the Mountain Bell case.

The American Telephone & Telegraph Company, along with a number of regional telephone companies, has announced plans to undercut companies that make a profit on these adult messages. The constitutional guarantee of free speech prevents telephone companies from refusing to transmit messages, no matter what the content. But the companies say that there is no requirement that a Dial-it message show a profit.

The steps to curb the adult messages range from AT&T's call-blocking service to a refusal to provide billing and collection services to the vendors of adult messages. "We are not denying them access," said Dick MacKnight, a spokesman for US West, one of the regional telephone companies. "We are denying them billing. If they want to continue offering those services, they are going to have to find a way to bill and collect."

Various citizens groups, including the Consenting Adults Telephone Rights Association in New York and Cable Communications in Los Angeles have presently filed suits that challenge a new federal law that bans "indecent" telephone programs. They argue that the ban is an unconstitutional intrusion on the freedom of speech. But the new law applies only to interstate calls. Thus, Dial-it programs will largely remain a problem for states and telephone companies to solve.[16]

CHAPTER

7

VIOLENCE AND VIDEOTAPE

Nearly 1,500 ten- to eleven-year-olds from thirty-four schools in Australia who had video cassette recorders (VCRs) at home were surveyed recently. The children were asked to describe a scene they had seen that was "so enjoyable that you always seem to remember it." This is what they wrote:

"I like the part . . .

where the man takes the heart out of another man" (Indiana Jones and the Temple of Doom).

when the teacher cuts the punk's arm off with the saw" (Class of '84).

where the girl chopped off her dad's head and ate it as a birthday cake" (Friday the 13th).

when the killer chops a lady into a hundred pieces" (Texas Chainsaw Massacre).

when all the people get killed and speared, stabbed, and pulled apart" (Turkey Shoot).

A 1987 study, by the National Coalition on Television Violence, of video cassette rentals in the United States learned the following about this medium. Fifty percent of all VCR rentals were of films that contained a great deal of violence, with extreme sexual, military, and revenge violence very common. NCTV called sadistic violence "a part of the education of modern American children and an issue of serious public concern."[1]

Some groups object to the fact that "splatter" movies are found in the horror section of most video stores. Even though they are not supposed to be seen by people under seventeen years old, they are rented freely to children in elementary school and watched at "gross-out" parties. Mutilation and repetitive acts of gore and violence are only part of the special effects that, many feel, have negative effects on viewers.

Writers of horror movies hold that they are just giving audiences what they want. Audiences want a body count of a dozen or so murders, they say. Besides, the argument goes, the violence is largely tongue-in-cheek and not to be taken seriously. In this changing world, they believe, things are far worse than what is shown on the VCR.

BACKGROUND

VCRs were first introduced to the American market in 1975. Right now they are found in nearly 40 percent of homes. By the year 1995, an estimated 85 percent of homes will own a VCR unit.[2] "This seven billion dollar industry pervades every dimension of our lives. There are more stores selling pornographic videos than there are McDonald hamburger stands."[3]

Originally, most people used their VCRs for recording broadcast and cable television programs that they were not able to watch at their scheduled times. But by 1979, consumers started seeking prerecorded tapes. Before long, there were thousands of video titles on the market, mostly of old movies. As time went on, the videos were divided into separate categories, including "Action Adventure," "Science Fiction," and "Horror." These three made up more than half of the videos available and often tended toward the pornographic, featuring scenes of explicit sex and brutal violence.

The development of VCRs made it more convenient than ever to bring films and other pornographic material into the home. If shown in theaters, many of these movies would have received ratings of "R" or "X" by the MPAA. But at the video stores, an estimated 60 percent of the cassette jackets do not list ratings.[4] Of the films without a rating on the packaging, many never obtained a rating in the first place, or the film was made just for the home video market.

The Junior Leagues in the United States, among other groups, are concerned about the growing problem of violence on videotapes. A survey by the leagues of ten- to thirteen-year-old children in New York found that the average child watches four R-rated VCR movies per month, with slasher movies the most popular. Although 50 percent of the films carry R or X ratings, the audience is predominantly under the age of eighteen.[5]

Illinois, Georgia, Maryland, and Tennessee currently require that video cassette packages carry ratings. Similar legislation has been proposed in at least nine other states, including New York and New Jersey. Right now, though, the laws do not apply to films that were not submitted to the MPAA ratings board. And it is these films, consisting largely of horror films, that alarm parents the most.

"If you're going to make a quickie, rip-off movie, you don't have to get a rating because you don't have that much money invested in it," said Jenny Pomeroy of Bronxville, New York, who heads an effort by the Junior Leagues to have such films clearly labeled. "All you need [to turn a profit] is a thousand people to rent it in a video store."[6]

In addition, many video outlets also have material available similar to what might be shown in an "adults-only" theater or in "peep" shows. The problem is made worse, critics say, because so many children are attracted by the forbidden and by the shocking and disgusting. When children go to the video stores, they are just as likely to bring home a tape "about Santa Claus slicing people up" as anything else.[7]

Producers are making more movies available on video for a couple of reasons. First, the cost of producing a sixty- to ninety-minute movie on video, about $10,000, is much less than shooting the same movie on film, about $75,000. Second, productions made on video tape can be edited and viewed in a matter of days, as compared to the weeks it may take to process and edit a film.

In September 1986, Dr. Kenneth Wooden, founder and president of the National Coalition for Children's Justice, met with over 2,100 schoolchildren in Reading, Pennsylvania, to discuss the prevalence of child abuse. He was told by more than 80 percent that they have access to "any and all the videoporn [sexually violent material] they want." The titles of videos that the children mentioned most often included *Debbie Does Dallas* and *Taboo I* and *Taboo II;* the last two deal very openly with incest. Children are exposed to such videos, he says, when they are rented by parents, older brothers and sisters, older friends, and neighbors.

Recent clinical observations by Dr. Victor Cline and others have indicated that children are finding and viewing their parents' videos and are experimenting on younger children with what they have learned.[8] Many parents worry about the effects of such violence, or the combination of explicit sex and violence, on their children. As Susan Cooke Kittredge of Middlesex, Vermont, mother of five children, says, "The twelve-year-old generation has grown up with movies that accomplish little more than inuring them to violence and insensitivity. It's a violent, whodunit, special effects world." The result, she said, "is that kids are much more tough-skinned than I am."[9]

An Australian study of video cassette viewing habits reached some interesting conclusions. Many children are being seriously affected by the enormous number of intensely sadistic and violent videos that they are seeing at home. The exposure is developing in them an increasing appetite for violence. The report went on to say that many parents are unaware of the influence of violent and sexually degrading material on themselves and their children.

Another finding of the Australian study was that current film ratings do not take violence seriously enough. The ratings provide little or no warning that these materials have harmful effects on both children and adults. Many parents are intimidated by advertising and very strong pressures from their children to allow extremely sadistic and violent entertainment into their homes.[10]

VIDEOPORN:
THE CONTROVERSY

Some say that when "consenting adults" watch video cassettes at home, no one is being harmed. Privately, the viewers have the right to watch what they choose, they believe. According to the Attorney General's Commission on Pornography, public opinion shows "a greater willingness to impose restrictions on theater showing and magazine publication of sexual activities than on home videos."[11]

Such groups as Morality in Media object to the notion of allowing individuals free access to all kinds of materials. In one of their publications, they refer to the *Paris Theatre* v. *Slaton* decision, June 1973, which said:

> *We categorically disapprove of the theory that obscene films acquire constitutional immunity from state regulation simply because they are exhibited for consenting*

adults only. Rights and interests other than those of the advocates are involved. These include the interest of the public in the quality of life, the total community, environment, the tone of commerce, and possibly, the public safety itself.[12]

Videoporn, the antiporn groups say, is no different from other pornography. The same obscenity laws should apply to video cassettes as to any other presentation of obscenity, in whatever medium it is produced. That the videos are viewed in the privacy of the home is irrelevant, since the obscenity laws are not aimed at the private individual but at the commercial distributor of illegal materials. Or to put it another way, it is the merchant who sells or rents obscene videos who is breaking the law, not the individual.

Each community establishes its own standards and has a right to legislate to protect those standards. In fact, community standards are part of the test for obscenity as defined by the Supreme Court. The current definition is found in the case *Miller* v. *California* (1973). According to the Court decision, the three basic guidelines are:

1. Whether the average person, applying contemporary standards would find that the work, taken as a whole appeals to the prurient interest (in sex),

2. Whether the work depicts or describes sexual conduct in a particularly offensive way, and

3. Whether the work, taken as a whole, lacks serious literary, artistic, political, or scientific value.

These guidelines are anything but simple. Virtually every word and phrase in the *Miller* test has been analyzed, explained, and further clarified in countless legal opinions. Ultimately, it is up to juries or judges to decide what is obscene under the guidelines and put themselves in the place of the average person to determine and apply community standards. Judge Robert Bork has said: "One of the freedoms, the major freedom of the society, is the freedom to choose to have a public morality."[13]

VIOLENCE AND PORNOGRAPHY: ARE THEY RELATED?

Many people think that violence is inherent in all pornography. Witnesses who appeared before the Attorney General's Commission on Pornography and those who submitted statements reported being physically beaten and psychologically abused in the course of being filmed for pornographic movies and videos. Some described how the young women and girls involved in pornography were sometimes tortured to the point of suffering permanent physical damage. One young man told how he was tied up with ropes and chains in various ways in order to be photographed.

An FBI agent told the Attorney General's Commission of the longtime heavy violence associated with the pornography industry. He told of very well-known names in the industry who had reported threats against them or physical brutality.

A bookstore operator associated with members of organized-crime families, describing the "discipline" within the pornography industry for those who disobeyed the rules on pricing, territory, and other matters, told this story: ". . . Bonjay, a year and half ago, took one of the guys, held him by his arms up against the wall in the alley, and it's common knowledge, the car ran into him with the front bumper up against the wall and shattered his knee. That's pretty good discipline." The same witness also reported bombs being thrown into stores that were not complying with the general price agreements or who failed to pay a tax to the organized-crime families.[14]

In addition to physical harm, there is evidence of a close connection between pornographic materials and murder. In October 1979, Michael George Thevis, who was then one of America's most notorious pornographers, was convicted in U.S. District Court for the Northern District of Georgia for violations of the Racketeer Influenced and Corrupt Organizations Act (RICO), violations that included murder along with arson and extortion. Robert DeSalvo, a leading distributor of the film *Deep Throat*, has been missing since January 1976 and is presumed to have been murdered. And Patsy Ricciardi was murdered in July 1985, just prior to the commission's hearings, presumably because of his dealings in the pornography business.

Some of the crimes reported to the commission actually appeared to have been patterned after the fictional assaults depicted in the pornographic material. To take a recent example, a college student was raped in her dormitory room by a fellow student while watching a pornographic movie. The defendant handcuffed and then sexually attacked her.[15]

Among the conclusions reached by the commission is that the "pornography industry systematically violates human rights with apparent impunity. . . . So that pornography can be made, victims have been exploited under conditions providing them a lack of choice and have been coerced to perform sex acts against their will. . . . Unwilling individuals have been forced to consume pornography, in order to pressure or induce or humiliate or browbeat them into performing the acts depicted. . . . Acts of physical aggression more and more appear tied to the targeting of women and children for sexual abuse in these materials."[16]

To support their view, the commission cites many instances where exposure to obscene material was linked to the acting out of violent sexual acts, involvement with criminal groups, and more. Take the case of two brothers, ages nine and ten, who discovered their parents' hard-core porno videotapes and played them repeatedly while the parents were at work. Based on what they saw on these videos, they proceeded to sexually abuse two younger boys, ages six and eight. They forced the young children to view the video cassettes and perform the activities they saw on the film. This sexual abuse went on for several years without the parents' knowledge.

The commission's report also makes the point that the stores where pornography is sold breed and attract crime. Such outlets for obscenity, they say, encourage sex-related crimes. When a thriving adult bookstore moves into a neighborhood, prostitution, narcotics, and street crime typically proliferate.

Some of the fastest and biggest money to be made in pornography is in adult peep shows. Typically, the customer pays a quarter to see a two-minute segment of film shown in a special machine in an adult bookstore. One of the most popular of these films is called *First Communion*. It shows an exceedingly violent attack by a motorcycle gang on a group of young girls receiving communion in a church.[17]

Law-enforcement officers find evidence of growing violence between rival criminal gangs struggling for control of the pornography industry. During the late 1970s, a number of persons involved with pornography were murdered in what were believed to be porno turf wars.

Item: The son of Joseph Periano, a producer of the porno film *Deep Throat*, and an innocent woman were murdered gangland style.

Item: In 1984, three men were shot to death and two wounded in a pornographic bookstore before it was set on fire.

Item: Two adult bookstores in Chicago were fire-bombed in November 1986.

Item: In December 1986 a man who tried to open an adult bookstore in Dallas was shot to death.

Since early 1970, members of the Colombo, Bonanno, Gambino, and DeCavalcante crime families have been establishing pornography operations in California. They used extortion and violence to help gain control over independent pornographers and built up a distribution network for pornographic materials. Central to their efforts are video cassettes. With the increase in numbers of VCRs came a growing demand for adult videotapes. Very quickly, pornographers, with links to the organized-crime families, entered this market, forming companies to produce, duplicate, distribute, and sell adult videotapes.

Experts believe that organized crime now controls more than 85 percent of all commercially produced pornography in the United States.[18] The sale and distribution of these materials produce huge profits for the crime lords, who also sell illegal drugs and engage in murder and other serious crimes. Perhaps even more harmful to society are the 7 billion (or more) tax-free dollars that organized crime receives each year from the pornography industry.

In trying to determine whether there is a connection between the pornography industry and organized crime, the Attorney General's Commission heard from a large number of law-enforcement personnel, members of organized-crime groups, people who worked in various phases of the pornography industry, and many legal sources. One retired veteran FBI agent, for instance, said that the distribution of pornography depended on the consent of organized crime. He added that the porno trade attracts these crime families because "it's a fast way of making a buck."

The owner of an adult bookstore described what happened to a man who went from New York to Atlanta with some porno films that he tried to sell on his own:

They found him at the [Atlanta] airport, with a $5,000 Rolex watch on and about eight grand in his pocket, and four rolls of film in his hands, with his head blown up in the trunk of his car. Nobody robbed him, nobody took a dime off him. They didn't even take the film. But he was at the airport with a New York ticket shoved in his coat pocket. Don't come down from New York selling unless you've been sent down.[19]

The commission concluded that there is indeed a connection between pornography and organized crime. They did admit, however, that they reached their conclusions in the face of a negative conclusion by the 1970 commission. The results also differed from evidence provided by the FBI; while several FBI offices reported some involvement by members and associates of organized crime, most offices had no verifiable information on the role of organized crime in the manufacture of pornography.

The commission's report of a link between some sexually explicit materials and violence led to an "all-out campaign against the distribution of obscene material" by Attorney General Edwin Meese III. Civil liberties groups said that the Justice Department's efforts to control the sale of sexually explicit materials by bringing indictments under the Racketeer Influenced and Corrupt Organizations statute (RICO) threatens First Amendment freedoms. This 1970 law, which has been used against organized-crime figures and drug traffickers, allows the Justice Department to seize assets derived from a racketeering activity. Under RICO, the Justice Department is permitted to seize *all* assets of bookstore or video shops, even if only a small number of books or videos are found to be obscene.[20]

In the first test case brought under the RICO statute, a Virginia couple was convicted in November 1987 of violating federal obscenity laws. The couple, Dennis and

Barbara Pryba, were owners of adult bookstores and video rental shops, with an estimated $1 million in assets. Even though a jury had found that relatively few items sold in their shops were obscene according to local standards, as required by a 1973 Supreme Court decision, the entire contents of their shops were confiscated.

H. Robert Showers, executive director of the Justice Department's National Obscenity Enforcement Unit, said it was proper to seek the assets of a racketeer, whether the criminal be a drug trafficker or a distributor of obscenity. "If you were selling drugs out of a bookstore, the bookstore would be sold and confiscated and forfeited," he said. "Under the law, you follow the same procedure if the bookstore owner is violating the law by selling legally obscene material."[21]

The idea is appalling to civil libertarians. They argue that the forfeiture could be used to seize the assets of legitimate shops that sell relatively few items of sexually explicit material. The result, they say, would be self-censorship by retailers fearing prosecution. "These cases lead to the suppression of material which we should presume—and in our system of government must be presumed—to be protected by the First Amendment," says Barry Lynn, legislative counsel for the American Civil Liberties Union.[22]

In March 1984 Indiana officials invoked the state's racketeering law against three adult bookstores in Fort Wayne, padlocking them and seizing their inventories. The Supreme Court agreed to review the case to determine whether the First Amendment bars the federal and state governments from using racketeering laws to close down bookstores selling materials a judge considers obscene. On February 21, 1989, the justices unanimously ruled that seizing adult bookstore publications before a court has found any of them to be obscene is prohibited by the First Amendment.

RECOMMENDATIONS

The 1984 Attorney General's Task Force on Family Violence determined that the evidence is "becoming overwhelming" that both normal children and adults are harmed by diets of violent entertainment. Yet, one study of adults in Canada and the United States found that only 3 percent realized that they were harmfully affected by exposure to violence in video cassettes and movies. And surveys by the NCTV have led to findings that the large majority of nine- and ten-year-old children are fully aware of which television programs and films are violent and which ones aren't. But neither the children nor their parents accept the idea that violence is an unhealthy means of entertainment.

On this basis, the NCTV recommends placing violence rating labels on all video cassettes. This kind of labeling, they believe, would avoid any charge of censorship but at the same time would identify the intensely violent films, such as *Indiana Jones and the Temple of Doom* and *Conan the Destroyer*, both of which earned PG ratings from the MPAA.

Various groups in the United States, along with the NCTV, are working to pass video-cassette bills in all the states that don't have such regulations. This legislation would require the tape producers or distributors to submit the tapes for MPAA ratings, to add educational labels, and to keep unrated and X-rated videos separate from the others. One of the goals is also to assign ratings to the older films, those made before 1968.

The state of Illinois already has such legislation. Yet, a recent NCTV study of Illinois video stores found 38 percent of all videos had no rating. About half of those, though, were unrated because they were produced before 1968.

A survey of Canadian attitudes regarding pornography in the media released in July 1985 reveals some interesting recommendations for videos and for movies in theaters. Those who responded supported uniform restrictions on explicit sex and violence, no matter whether the films were meant to be shown in public theaters or at home on VCRs.[23]

In regard to the recommended restrictions on video cassettes for home use, a majority of all age groups (*except* the twelve- to seventeen-year-olds) recommended banning sexually violent material completely. However, only 29 percent of the twelve- to seventeen-year-olds recommended such a ban.

The results were surprisingly similar to the results of a recent *Newsweek* magazine poll of Americans conducted by the Gallup organization. Of those polled, 68 percent felt that theaters should be prohibited from showing movies that depict sexual violence, and 63 percent felt that the sale or rental of video cassettes featuring sexual violence should be banned. Curiously enough, even more, 73 percent, felt that magazines that show sexual violence should be banned.[24]

Several countries around the world are making efforts to deal with the harmful effects of violent entertainment. In England, certain of the most intensely violent videos, such as *The Evil Dead,* are totally banned. In Canada, the Canadian Association of Broadcasters is sponsoring public-service announcements to warn viewers of the dangers of entertaining oneself with violent or sexually degrading material. In New Zealand, the Mental Health Foundation has obtained a commitment from the government that it will start cutting down on the high levels of violence present on New Zealand's government-controlled television.

Several groups interested in curbing the violence in video cassettes are calling for four major steps:

1. Stricter film ratings that pay more attention to the violence content of the videos.

2. Requirements that intensely violent and sadistic videos be rated X and not be made available for home viewing.

3. Restrictions on R-rated videos so that they be available for adult rental only. Also, that they carry a warning stating that researchers have determined that violent and sexually degrading entertainment has harmful unconscious effects on both children and adult viewers. In addition, the Australian Children's Council recommends that the label read, "It is an offense to show this videotape to any person between the ages of two and eighteen years."

4. Establishment of an M rating that carries a warning against violence and a statement along the lines of, "This video is considered to be unsuitable for showing to children below the age of fifteen and may contain material harmful to older viewers as well."

CHAPTER

RECORDS AND
MUSIC VIDEOS

■ *Young children reportedly had nightmares for a week after watching the music video* Thriller, *in which Michael Jackson turns into a monster.*[1]

■ *In California, an estimated 50,000 teens in the Los Angeles area alone belong to gangs; many are said to be organized around heavy-metal and punk-rock bands.*[2]

■ *Blackie Lawless of the heavy-metal band W.A.S.P. says that he likes drinking blood out of a skull and torturing females on stage.*[3]

■ *Motley Crue's music video* Looks That Kill *shows women in cages being attacked by a male band clad in studded leather. At the end of the video, a laser-shooting woman frees them and sets the band on fire.*[4]

■ *In Billy Idol's music video* Dancing with Myself, *the star blows people off a building with bolts of electricity. A man sharpens a straight-edge razor as if to kill a naked woman who is in chains behind a translucent sheet.*[5]

■ Rock School, *a music video by the group Heaven, features a principal wearing a stocking mask and a school guard menacing students with a vicious Doberman dog.*[6]

■ *Bon Jovi's* Runaway *features a miniskirted girl rebelling against her parents and finally burning them alive.*[7]

■ *In a concert by the band Lizzy Borden, a band member puts a woman into a coffin and strikes the box with an ax. He then drinks the "blood" that spurts into the air and spits it out at the audience.*[8]

Rock music first emerged on the national scene in the 1950s. Thirty years later, rock had become mainstream and immensely popular. The recording industry produces some 2,500 rock albums annually and sells millions and millions of copies.[9]

In 1985, a powerful group of parents persuaded some record companies to put warning labels on albums that were deemed offensive. They argued that parents have a right to know about the sex and violence content of the music their children buy. According to them, some rock music is tied to witchcraft, death, and suicide. As such, it contributes to a rise in teen suicides and other kinds of violence among young people.

Preachers and politicians jumped into the fray. Rev. Jimmy Swaggart denounced Wal-Mart stores in a televised sermon condemning rock music. As a result, the 900 stores in the chain were ordered to remove certain records and rock magazines from their shelves.

Opposed to any ban on rock are those who say that the critics are attempting to curb free speech. Any attempt to label or limit rock lyrics, they say, is censorship. The lyrics, violent or not, have little or no effect on listeners, they say. "The . . . knee-jerk overreactive surge of antimusic mania, fueled by preachers, 'concerned parents,' and exploitive politicians may seem like something dreadfully new," writes Leo N. Miletich, but "the hysteria is as old as music itself."[10]

The latest style of music to enter the mainstream of American culture is rap music—rhythmic, rhymed chanting to a driving beat. Like rock 'n' roll, the influence of rap can now be found in all parts of the nation's media. According to industry estimates, between 1984 and 1988 stores have sold $240 million worth of rap records and tapes. And fans have spent $50 million to see rap groups in concert.

Rap's sound can be aggressive and its message a call to rebel against authority. Some parents and critics have attacked the music's sexual explicitness, macho swaggering, and association with violence. When the movie made by the rap group Run-D.M.C., *Krush Groove*, was released, violence broke out at several theaters. Now violence seems to be a part of some concert performances of rap music, as well.

ROCK ALBUMS
AND CONCERTS

Some critics call songs with lyrics that focus on the gruesome and that promote violence "dark rock." Others call it "heavy metal." But whatever the music is called, this type of rock generally sells anywhere from 250,000 to 400,000 copies.[11] Between record sales, concert tours, and music videos, the music reaches very substantial numbers of fans.

First played in England about twenty years ago, heavy-metal rock became very closely associated with the countercultural rebellion. At first, many of the songs were political. In time, the music turned more morbid and dealt with such subjects as devil worship, sadistic sex, murder, rape, and suicide. Just a list of some of the names of the dark-rock and heavy-metal bands shows their fascination with violence, sex, and the power of evil: Venom, the Dead Kennedys, Suicidal Tendencies, Warlord, Predator, the Scorpions, and Slayer.

Male rock star Alice Cooper, an early proponent of

"shock rock," used props such as a guillotine to cut off the head of a mannequin and giant live boa constrictor snakes to excite his audiences. The band Kiss took Cooper's violence one step further by using grotesque makeup and outrageous costumes. Ozzy Osbourne, formerly the lead vocalist for the heavy-metal band Black Sabbath, is reputed to have once bit off the head of a live bat during a performance.

The album covers are equally violent. The cover of the Exciters' album *Violence & Force,* for instance, depicts a woman desperately trying to hold shut a door while a killer thrusts both hands, one holding a dagger, the other dripping blood, through the open crack.

Rock album and concert promotional material show Blackie Lawless of W.A.S.P. supposedly drinking blood out of a human skull, an act he used to perform on stage. The stage sets of some of these bands include torture racks, skulls, and ghouls. W.A.S.P. has used skeletons, axes, and blades, along with gallons of fake blood, in their act. Their publicity has shown a bloodied, half-naked woman chained to a torture rack. Some performances have simulated attacks and acts of torture inflicted on a woman.

In an October 1985 article in the fan magazine *Hit Parader,* Blackie Lawless said: "To me rock is theater, electric vaudeville. . . . It's the place where you can do just about anything and get away with it. It's a zone where rules and restrictions are just totally thrown out the window."[12]

Magazines aimed at rock music fans also promote gory entertainment. In one magazine article about his W.A.S.P. band, Lawless told writer Keith Greenberg that "nastiness" is central to the W.A.S.P. performance. "I don't mean vulgar 'nasty,' " he said. "I mean violent. We sound like a tin can ripped open with your hands, that kind of nasty. It doesn't leave a clean cut."[13]

The messages in heavy metal can be violent. Some heavy-metal songs stress the torture, rape, and murder of women. Young people are also portrayed as victims of brutal violence by some of these bands. One group, the Dead Kennedys, has a song called "I Kill Children." The words are: "I kill children,/I love to see them die./I kill children,/I make their mothers cry." And in their song "Kill Again," another band, Slayer, sings: "Kill the preacher's only son/Watch the infant die/Bodily dismemberment/Drink the purest blood."[14]

THE MUSIC VIDEO

Putting music and pictures together, as in music videos, is an idea that goes back to the cartoons of the 1930s and 1940s that were made to songs of Cab Calloway and Louis Armstrong. And in 1943, some jukeboxes in nightclubs and diners let viewers hear songs and watch the performers on miniscreens. Rock videos were first shown in European clubs during the 1970s. But the real success came with the advent of cable television.

The Music Television Video (MTV) channel started in 1981. It was successful right away. Within three years, MTV was reaching into more than 22 million households.[15] Since then, twenty-four-hour-a-day music-video channels have increased rapidly. This rock-music television channel airs many videos that are considered more violent and sexually explicit than other television shows.

It may be too soon to judge the impact of music videos on popular culture. Music videos now reach vast audiences, particularly the young, not only on television but also in video bars and discos. Some motion-picture theaters show videos before the feature films, and a number of shopping malls, record shops, and department stores show them to attract customers. And, of course, they are available for VCR viewing. In short, music videos are now within the reach of virtually everyone.

Music videos are essentially three- to five-minute vignettes that illustrate popular recordings. They are of two basic kinds: performance videos, which show the artists performing in concert or studio settings; and concept videos, which project images of actors and actresses that interpret or embellish the words and meaning of the song.

Professors Barry L. Sherman and Joseph R. Dominick of the University of Georgia analyzed 366 videos—200 performance videos and 166 concept videos. They found that episodes of violence occurred in 93 (56 percent) of the concept videos. On average, videos with violence contained about three separate aggressive acts. Men made up nearly three-fourths of the aggressors; victims of violence were even more likely to be female and young. Hand-to-hand combat was the most common form of aggression in the music video. Based on the results, the study concluded that videos are "violent, male-oriented, and laden with sexual content."[16]

Concept videos receive most of the criticism for being sexist and violent. As a Los Angeles music critic put it, ". . . Women are depicted as monstrous Amazonian beauties out of a Richard Linder nightmare surrounded by slow-motion mayhem and implied violence."[17] Often "they play on Naziesque sadomasochistic fetishes." As an example, the *Flesh for Fantasy* video shows Billy Idol in a stormtrooper outfit strutting around and giving Hitler's Nazi salute. The world shown in these videos is often one of "cosmic threat and magical power. . . . The trigger is all-powerful acts of destruction and salvation."[18]

Because a bold image is a crucial part of music videos, there is much stereotyping of both men and women. Favorite male images include sailors, thugs, and rough-looking gang members. The females are either whores or goddesses, queens or servants. Feminists have frequently denounced the false images of women as shown in the videos.

How do music videos compare to some of the other media? The video may be thought of as a kind of cross between television, radio, film, and a stereo record. The video is like television, because it tells a story and is watched sporadically, like soap operas, sitcoms, and televised sporting events.

like radio, because listeners do other things while the song plays.

like film, because it is often watched in groups.

like a stereo record, because a recording is, in fact, the basis for almost every music video.

Usually, the videos evoke an intense euphoria in listeners, a kind of dreamy "high." A survey of 603 students, grades nine to twelve, in an ethnically mixed high school in San Jose, California, were asked why they watch videos. They said videos

give "more meaning" to a song than they themselves could conjure up.

give "different perspectives" on the meaning.

"get me mellow."

"lift me up and get me violent!"

"make me feel like a dream."[19]

Tipper Gore, founder of the Parents' Music Resource Center, has said that videos by heavy-metal rock groups, such as Motley Crue and Twisted Sister, frequently feature what she called "exceptional savagery with special effects that leave nothing to the imagination."[20]

The National Coalition of Television Violence, among other groups, has criticized what they consider the especially senseless violence and violence between men and women in music videos. They see it as a virtual prescription to violence in life. The videos, they say, use violence not as action but as atmosphere and a tranquilizer. George Gerbner, speaking of the violence in music videos, agrees that many videos convey a mood of defiance and insensitivity. The medium evokes sensations that are far removed from any feelings of social responsibility.

Dr. Thomas Radecki, chairman of the NCTV and a psychiatrist at the University of Illinois School of Medicine, estimates that 45 percent of over a thousand rock videos he surveyed were of a violent nature. A large number were rated extremely violent. In interviews with college students, Dr. Radecki found a high degree of desensitization among individuals who watch violent videos.

Some other research projects also point up this view of the harmful effects of violent music-video entertainment. Drs. Susan Reilly and Sharas Rehman of Miami University in Oxford, Ohio, concluded an important study of violent music videos. They found that students became somewhat more desensitized to violence after viewing only a few violent videos. Dr. Rehman completed a similar study of over a hundred college students at Pennsylvania State University and found similar results.[21]

One example that is used to illustrate the harmful results of a music video is the Twisted Sister video *We're Not Gonna Take It*. It tells of a boy who rebels against his angry father and finally throws his father through a window. When a young man in New Mexico murdered his father in the same way, a number of commentators believed that this tragedy was inspired by the Twisted Sister video.

Dr. Radecki notes that music-video violence is not necessarily more violent than that seen on prime-time television. But he emphasizes the need to consider four "key factors" when dealing with violent music videos:

1. Studies by the U.S. Surgeon General and others that have provided "overwhelming evidence that violence on prime-time television has important harmful effects on normal children and adult viewers."

2. Music videos appeal to adolescents and preadolescents, who have less ability than adults to understand the potentially harmful effects of violent entertainment.

3. Music videos include more violence between the sexes and more sadistic violence than does prime-time television.

4. Viewers have no idea what to expect on MTV; they may, at any time, suddenly see images of violence, sadism, and callous sexual portrayals.

"Despite overwhelming evidence of harm," says Dr. Radecki, "there are no warnings of harm, and no non-violent, non-degrading alternatives in rock music video entertainment."[22]

Nevertheless, Marshall Cohen, the senior vice-president of MTV, remains a staunch defender of music videos. He asserts that they must conform to stringent standards before being considered for broadcast. "We think if they make it through the standards they should be on MTV," says Cohen. Music videos were bound to spark protests, he claims, because "rock 'n' roll has always been somewhat rebellious and on the edge."[23]

THE "ROCK (OR RAP) MUSIC IS HARMFUL" ARGUMENT

No one seriously considers rock music the sole cause of increased violence in our society. But many do believe that the messages of the music, which are largely aimed at children, promote and glorify violence. Thus, some regard them as contributing to the problem.

In October 1987, Surgeon General Dr. C. Everett Koop warned that explicit sexual and violent imagery in rock music has a bad influence on children and adolescents— one that could lead to suicide, satanism, and drug and alcohol abuse. Dr. Koop said that many videos combine senseless violence and senseless pornography to the beat of rock music.

Dr. Joseph Stuessy, professor of music at the University of Texas at San Antonio and author of *The Heavy Metal User's Manual*, makes the point that all music affects moods, emotions, attitudes, and behavior. Heavy-metal music, which he differentiates from other forms of popular music and from mainstream rock 'n' roll, is no exception. Heavy metal, he says, celebrates extreme violence, substance abuse, explicit sex, satanism, and hatred. "I know personally of no form of popular music before which has had hatred as one of its central themes," he writes. "Anyone who says, 'I can listen to heavy metal, but it doesn't affect me' is simply wrong. It simply affects different people in different degrees and different ways." [24]

Advertisers know that endorsement of products by rock stars helps sales. Michael Jackson's Pepsi commercials, for example, boosted sales by an estimated $20 million. If the commercials sell products, experts believe, certainly the music videos themselves—which are promoting violence—will have much more influence.

Many professionals who study adolescent behavior have investigated the effects of dark rock on their patients. Dr. David Guttman, professor of psychiatry at Northwestern University, has said: "Rock has so often been involved in these things [violence, teen suicide, etc.], many of us in psychiatry have had to take it more seriously." [25]

Dr. Paul King, medical director of the adolescent program at Charter Lakeside Hospital in Memphis, Tennessee, reports that over 80 percent of the adolescent patients he treats in a psychiatric facility have listened to heavy-metal music for several hours a day. He notes that for these patients, the song lyrics become a way of life, a kind of religion.

At the time that the NCTV released its music-video report, Dr. Radecki expressed concern about the growing emphasis of violence in rock music. He criticized the message that he finds in this music—that violence is normal, that hostile sexual relations between men and women are common and acceptable, and that heroes torture and murder others for fun. He stated:

I have already seen several cases of young people in my psychiatric practice with severe problems of anger and anti-social behavior who are deeply immersed into a subculture of violent rock music. . . . It is plainly obvious that they are heavily immersed in fantasies of violence, that also are affecting their way of thinking and their behavior in an anti-social direction.[26]

A mother in San Antonio, Texas, described a tragedy that she attributed to the hypnotic influence of rock music. One night during the summer of 1980, her sixteen-year-old son was unable to sleep because of his allergies and a severe headache. According to her testimony, the boy decided to listen to Pink Floyd's album *The Wall*. Suddenly, he got up and moved steadily in the direction of his aunt, who was asleep on a couch. Within moments, he had attacked and killed her.

A related incident is said to have occurred in May 1986. Newspapers widely covered an incident in which a twenty-year-old boy raped his mother and then brutally murdered her with an ax and a pair of scissors. The defense pleaded that the influence of satanism and heavy-metal music caused the boy to commit this heinous crime.

Many educators feel that teenage suicides are linked to depression aggravated by fatalistic music and lyrics. One example is nineteen-year-old John McCollum, who shot himself in the head at his home in Indio, California, on October 27, 1984. The teenager had been listening to the albums of Ozzy Osbourne, a British heavy-metal rock star, just before he died. In fact, he was still wearing stereo headphones when his body was discovered. The lyrics of "Suicide Solution" are part of what McCollum's parents claim was responsible for the teenager's suicide.

The boy's father sued Osbourne and his two record companies, CBS Records and Jet Records. McCollum said that CBS had released the records knowing that they could promote suicide. Osbourne denied the charge and insisted that the parents had misinterpreted his lyrics. Far from being a song written for suicide, Osbourne said, it was antisuicide.

The song, according to Osbourne, warns that alcohol can become a suicide solution if it gets out of control. His song, he continued, is "about living, not dying. People who really listen know that. The others—well, I can't do anything about them. I'm not going to stop making music because they won't listen." Finally, Osbourne said, "it's a bigger tragedy no one recognized his [John McCollum's] real problems went far deeper than music."[27] A trial judge dismissed the suit on grounds that the lyrics are protected by the First Amendment.

Jean and Elmer Fisk of San Pablo, California, are two more parents who believe the song "Suicide Solution" had something to do with their son's death in October 1985:

> When my husband and I were going through his papers after he died, we found the words to a rock song, "Suicide Solution." We asked his girl friend about the words and she told us it was his favorite song. I feel that these words opened up a tragic alternative to him that he would not have otherwise considered.[28]

Among the many accounts of suicide deaths attributed to violent songs of heavy-metal bands are the following:

Item: His parents said that sixteen-year-old Steve Boucher was so obsessed with songs like the AC/DC hit "Shoot to Thrill" that he shot himself under the band's poster-calendar, which hung on the wall in his room.

Item: Dennis Bartts, also sixteen, hanged himself from the goalposts of the football field at the Center Point, Texas, High School while listening to AC/DC's "Highway to Hell" on his cassette tape recorder.

Item: Philip Morton hanged himself from a closet door in his home in Delafield, Wisconsin, in February 1986. Police found a human skull and a burning candle near the body and a tape of Pink Floyd's album *The Wall*. The album, which includes the songs "Is There Anybody Out There?," "Goodbye Cruel World," and "Waiting for the Worms," had been playing continuously.

Item: Raymond Belknap, an eighteen-year-old from Sparks, Nevada, shot himself to death in a double suicide pact. His friend, who survived a severe wound to the face, said the music of the heavy-metal rock group Judas Priest lulled them into thinking that "the answer to life is death." In late 1988, the Nevada Supreme Court decided that the parents could sue the band because of the alleged effect of its music.

Some rock groups describe devil worshiping, or satanic practices, in great detail in their lyrics. The effect on teens, some believe, is to offer them a scheme for conducting a satanic ritual.

Cleo Wilson, a Denver, Colorado, detective and a specialist in occult crime, cites an increase in satanic activity over the past six years. In February 1986, she investigated a murder in which the victim had drunk his own blood. Her partner, cult expert Detective Bill Wickersham, estimates that animal slaughter and mutilation, in connection with such rituals, have increased by 50 percent over the past five years. Although many satanic rituals are generally against the law, satanism itself is protected by the First Amendment right to freedom of religion.

Detective Wickersham believes that the occultism in the music offers an escape from a violent world. He says that the message is fatalistic: The world is going to end, so take what you can now and hurt whoever gets in your way.

Heavy-metal rock has long been associated with the occult. According to Dann Cuellar, a television reporter in San Antonio who has investigated several satanic crimes, the link between kids and satanism is the music. In virtually every case, he claims, the names of the rock groups or their songs are connected to such atrocities. Cult expert Sandi Gallant, of the San Francisco Police Department, agrees. "No matter what heavy metal band leaders say," she asserts, "they are projecting an image to the kids that they are satanists. Children want to emulate their stars."[29]

Not long ago, seventeen-year-old Gary Lauwers was mutilated and murdered in Northport, New York. Spray-painted nearby were the names of Ozzy Osbourne and his former band, Black Sabbath, along with satanic symbols. The young man charged with the crime, Richard Kasso, reportedly was involved with drugs, seances, animal sacrifices, grave digging, and other satanic activities. The Lauwers' attorney spoke of a connection between the murder and the behavior of rock musicians.

Much of the violence associated with rock and rap music spills over into violence associated with such concerts:

Item: The single year 1986 was marked by a striking jump in the frequency and severity of violent incidents: On May 18, in Tacoma, Washington, during a rock concert, a nineteen-year-old man was killed in a knife attack and the assailant's sixteen-year-old girlfriend was also stabbed. On May 19, in Kalamazoo, Michigan, a woman was raped after attending a Judas Priest concert.

Item: During an August 1987 rap concert in Long Beach, California, about thirty persons were hurt and four others arrested for gang-related fights. And in November, a man was stabbed to death during a melee that followed a rap concert in New Haven, Connecticut.

Item: Perhaps the most notorious music-related violence occurred on September 10, 1988, when one man was stabbed to death by muggers who ripped a pendant from his neck during a rap concert. Fourteen other mugging victims were stabbed, beaten, or slashed with razors.

These outbreaks of violence and other incidents have led some patrons to file lawsuits against arenas and groups. For example, one woman filed a $5 million suit against the band Aerosmith because she had been punched in the face and suffered a broken nose. She claimed her injury was a direct result of the group's encouraging violence on stage and in their recordings. Other have claimed damages for robbery, assaults, and threats of murder.

In some cases, the arenas are fighting back. In an unprecedented move, New York City's Madison Square Garden, a popular site for concerts, sued several gang members for violent incidents, including terrorizing patrons. Other concert arenas have added security for heavy-metal concerts. Guards may "pat search" or ask patrons to open their handbags if they are suspected of carrying weapons.

THE "ROCK MUSIC IS JUST ENTERTAINMENT" ARGUMENT

Heads of record companies, as well as many other people, are opposed to any music censorship. Sharply critical of those who would ban rock 'n' roll or other forms of musical entertainment, they base their arguments on a range of evidence, from research studies to legal opinions.

A 1986 study by two professors at California State University at Fullerton clearly supports the view that rock music is not harmful. The researchers found that teens don't listen to the words of the songs, just to the beat. Parents, they say, hear more sophisticated themes in the songs than the children really understand.

Author Roger Desmond agrees that young people listen more to the beat than to the words of rock music. He writes: "In one study it was found that if you ask a high school student to tell you the story of his favorite song, he can't. What they're listening to is the beat, just like they said on 'American Bandstand.' "[30]

Ira Glasser, executive director of the American Civil Liberties Union, also opposes those who would censor rock music because of the lyrics. He finds their position objectionable for several reasons. First, he feels that only a few of the 10,000 songs released each year reflect violence. Of these, many come from records that are unsuccessful. Then, most song lyrics are far less explicit than books or movies. The songs, to be successful, must be played on the radio, a medium that prohibits explicit violence and sex far more than the other media.

All lyrics, Glasser says, should not be censored because of a few objectionable excerpts any more than all new fiction should be censored because of excerpts from obscure trash novels. To falsely brand all rock music as violent just lends support to those who would force music publishers to set up a rating system for records. Most rock lyrics, in fact, show little explicit depiction of violence, including sexual violence. Listeners rely on their own interpretations of lyrics. And since song lyrics, like poetry, can be interpreted many ways, listeners often attribute meanings to a song that the writer never intended.

Glasser points out that John Denver's "Rocky Mountain High" and Simon and Garfunkel's "Bridge Over Troubled Water" have been banned in some places by those who hear in the lyrics hidden references to drugs. Obviously, any rating system that is based on someone's interpretation would inevitably lead to restrictions on freedom of expression.

Once such censorship begins, music publishers would be forced for economic reasons to conform. Take, for example, the pressure on Wal-Mart stores to stop carrying rock records and magazines. The result is a narrowing of the range of permissible expression. And Glasser warns: "That is exactly how blacklisting began in the 1950's, not through legislation or blunt government censorship, but through economic intimidation organized by private pressure groups. . . . Rock music may not seem so important to adults. But millions of teenagers will be learning a terrible lesson about freedom of expression if we permit a system to be established that imposes taste and restricts songwriters based on the censorious feelings of adults with vivid imaginations."[31]

Those who object to any kind of censorship find that calls for bans on music are not actually anything new. As far back as the fourth century, the Greek historian Ephorus said, "Music was invented to deceive and delude mankind." Accordingly, what followed in later eras were just variations on this theme. In a *Short View of the Immorality and Profaneness of the English Stage*, Jeremy Collier (1650–1726) wrote: "Musick is almost as dangerous as Gunpowder; and it may be requires looking after. . . . 'Tis possible a publick Regulation might not be amiss."[32]

It is also very striking how strongly today's rock 'n' roll controversy resembles reactions against popular music in the United States during the 1930s. Take this headline in *Downbeat* magazine of December 1937: "Ellington Refutes Cry That Swing Started Sex Crimes."

The article, by prominent composer, pianist, and bandleader Duke Ellington, refuted charges that had been made against swing music by Arthur Cremin, an instructor at the New York School for Music. Cremin attributed the recent wave of sex crimes to the vogue for "hot" jazz. He had reportedly placed young men and young women in a room alone. First, he played symphonic recordings followed by a set of swing recordings. According to the teacher, couples became more familiar when the music turned to jazz.

Today's heroes, many say, are no worse than Duke Ellington, Benny Goodman, or Elvis Presley were in their day. Ragtime and swing music were each condemned in turn. Benny Goodman's music was labeled "a degenerated and demoralizing music system" by the archbishop of Dubuque, the Most Reverend Francis J. L. Beckman. He said the music had been "turned loose to gnaw away the moral fiber of young people. Jam sessions, jitterbugs and cannibalistic rhythmic orgies are wooing our youth along the primrose path to Hell!" he preached.[33]

Rock groups are familiar with the charge that their music promotes devil worship and disregard for human life. Yet offstage, many of these musicians have families and children. "Not one says he worships Satan. But the reputation lingers," writes David Hinckley.

Perhaps a basic attitude of rock musicians on the effects of rock music can be summed up in the words of heavy-metal rocker Nikki Sixx. When asked, "Do you ever have second thoughts about your influence on teenagers?" Sixx replied, "No. I think we have a positive message. It's very much an American message: Live free, express yourself, and it's up to the youth to change the world."[34]

ACTIONS TAKEN
As early as 1984, the National Congress of Parents and Teachers called on record companies to label their products for sexual content, violence, and profanity, in order to inform parents about inappropriate materials. In May 1985, Tipper Gore (wife of Tennessee senator Albert Gore) and the wives of a number of other government officials organized the PMRC. The group's purpose was to alert the public to the "worst excesses" in rock music aimed at the teenage market. PMRC believes that either parents are unaware of the trends in rock music or unsure of what they can do about them. By organizing, they hoped to pressure music-industry leaders to restrain themselves in producing what they call "porn rock."

Among the supporters of the PMRC are the American Academy of Pediatrics and the National Health Association. All these groups work to decrease the consumption of intensely violent rock, especially heavy-metal music.

Religious fundamentalist extremists have burned records, attempted to ban performances, and accused rock musicians of being tools of the devil. In one case, they claim that a group known as KISS stands for "Knights in Satan's Service."

Some fundamentalists believe that rock groups use a process they call "backward masking" to burn satanic messages into LPs, heard when records are played in reverse. A bill citing LPs by the Beatles, Pink Floyd, Electric Light Orchestra, Queen, and Styx and calling for the clear labeling of all records containing "backward masking" was unanimously passed by the lower house of the Arkansas legislature but rejected by the Senate. Legislation requiring the labeling of "embedded subliminal communications" has also been introduced in the California Assembly.[35]

Eddie Fritts, president of the National Association of Broadcasters (NAB), responded to the pressure groups by sending 800 station owners a letter alerting them to the growing concern of the public over rock records and music videos. He acknowledged that the sexually explicit and violent language of some recent rock records and their related music videos were becoming a matter of great concern.

Two weeks later, Fritts asked the heads of forty-five major record companies to protect the public by including copies of the songs' lyrics with all recordings. The June 1985 issue of the recording industry newspaper *Radio and Records* reported a generally favorable reaction. Many agreed it was a good idea to quiet the opposition by printing the words.

But most of the record companies objected to the NAB request. "It smells of censorship," said Lenny Waronker, president of Warner Brothers Records, to the *Los Angeles Times*. "Rock and roll over the years has always had these little . . . furors. Radio stations can make their own decisions about what they want to play."

And from a representative of a local California radio station: "It's freedom of choice. The music is the beat; the lyrics come secondary. . . . We make our money on sex, from A to Z. It's what sells."

On May 31, 1985, sixteen wives of U.S. representatives and senators met with Stan Gortikov of the Recording Industry Association of America (RIAA) and presented the following portion of a letter:

> *Because of the excesses that exist in the music industry today, we petition the industry to exercise voluntary self-restraint perhaps by developing guidelines and/or a rating system, such as that of the movie industry, for use by parents in order to protect our younger children from such mature themes.*[36]

The PMRC insists that it does not advocate a ban of any albums or tapes. But it does urge the use of warning labels and/or printed lyrics visible on the outside packaging of music products. They feel that the industry should consider itself responsible for their products' effect on young people. Says Mrs. Gore, "Adults must not overlook the exaggerated impact that violent and explicit images can have on children, or forget that children are different."

Advocates of labeling say that it is the parents' right to protect their children from explicit messages. That right, they feel, is just as valuable as the right of free speech to the artist. These two rights are not mutually exclusive, says Mrs. Gore, and one should not be sacrificed for the other. Providing ratings and lyrics on records, tapes, and videos, they point out, will help parents make better choices for their children.

In September 1985, a hearing was held before the Senate's Commerce Committee to investigate the prevalence of pornographic, violent rock lyrics. As a result of the hearing, PMRC agreed to the formation of an RIAA policy statement on explicit lyrics and put an end to the request for an R rating on albums or tapes in exchange for the warning "Explicit Lyrics—Parental Advisory."

As of this writing, the record companies rarely do affix such labels; only a dozen or so albums have been issued with labels or lyrics. Mrs. Gore has lobbied the Music Television Network to cluster violent or sexually explicit videos during evening hours, a suggestion that has not been accepted by the station.

There have been some efforts, too, to stop the disturbances that sometimes erupt after rock concerts. After the stabbing death following the previously mentioned rap concert in New Haven, Connecticut, in November 1987, officials changed the method of assigning seats. The decision they made was to treat the issue as a law-enforcement problem but not to discontinue the concerts.[37]

CONCLUSION

The conclusion one must draw from the evidence is that there is a great deal of violence in the media. First, newspapers, magazines, and books; then television and the movies; and now cable TV, videotapes, and music records and videos all include scenes of violence. Almost every one of us in America is exposed daily to representations—fictional and real—of murder, assault, stabbing, torture, rape, and more.

What, then, can we do about violence in the media? Will a program to "clean up" the media help slow the trend toward the increasing use of violence as a means of solving problems?

The answers are not easy, as we have already shown. Strong laws and regulations that control the free flow of information clash with the democratic notions of a free press and First Amendment guarantees.

Violence will be uprooted from our media only when we have a sharp turnabout in our national priorities, when we begin to move toward goals that will improve the quality of life in this nation—for example, the rebuilding of our cities, the reform of our courts and prisons, the improvement of the conditions of our poor and homeless. Then perhaps we will see an enrichment of our lives and our media. Unless this happens, the principal message we will continue to get from the media is that violence is an exciting, sometimes rewarding, and necessary part of life.

NOTES

PREFACE

[1]"The Age of Security," *New York Times* editorial, May 23, 1988, p. A18.

CHAPTER 1

[1]John Godwin, *Murder, USA: The Ways We Kill Each Other* (New York: Ballantine Books, 1978), p. 50.
[2]Newsletter of the National Coalition to Ban Handguns, May 1988.
[3]*The Hate Movement*, special report of the Anti-Defamation League (New York: Anti-Defamation League, 1986), p. 12.
[4]Godwin, p. 56.
[5]"U.S. Says Violent Crime Dropped," *New York Times*, May 9, 1988, p. A14.
[6]"Crime Reported to the Police Increased for 3rd Year," *New York Times*, April 17, 1988, p. 25.

[7] Robert Baker and Sandra Ball, *Mass Media and Violence*, vol. IX, *A Report to the National Commission on the Causes and Prevention of Violence* (Washington, DC: U.S. Government Printing Office, 1969), p. 235.

[8] Godwin, p. 50.

[9] Baker and Ball, p. 55.

[10] Hugh David Graham and Ted Robert Gurr, *Violence in America: Historical and Comparative Perspectives* (Washington, DC: U.S. Government Printing Office, 1969), p. 40.

[11] Elliott Currie, *Confronting Crime: An American Challenge* (New York: Pantheon, 1985), p. 444.

[12] James F. Kirkham, *Assassination and Political Violence: A Report to the National Commission on the Causes and Prevention of Violence* (New York: Praeger Publishers, 1970), p. 1.

[13] Sam Howe Verhovek, "A Week's Killings: A Profile of Violent Deaths in New York," *New York Times*, April 8, 1980, pp. B1, B4.

[14] Donald MacGillis, *Crime in America, The ABC Report* (Radnor, Pennsylvania: Chilton Book Company, 1983), p. 90.

[15] Tipper Gore, *Raising PG Kids in an X-rated Society* (Nashville, Tenn.: Abingdon Press, 1987), p. 45.

[16] "Los Angeles Dragnet Over Gang Violence Leads to 634 Arrests," *New York Times*, April 10, 1988, p. 30.

[17] Baker and Ball, p. 200.

[18] Verhovek, p. B5.

[19] Ibid.

[20] Ibid.

[21] Ibid.

[22] "Three Youths Shot on a Subway Train in Brooklyn," *New York Times*, April 5, 1988, p. B2.

[23] "Boy Convicted in Thrill Killing," *New York Times*, March 12, 1988, p. 9.

[24] Glenn Collins, "Violence of Workplace: Unseen Signs, Unexpected Explosions," *New York Times*, April 22, 1988, p. A15.

[25] Sarah Lyall, "Two Homeless Men Set Afire by Youths at a Bus Terminal," *New York Times*, January 20, 1988, p. B2.

[26] *1987 Audit of Anti-Semitic Incidents*, Summary report of Anti-Defamation League (New York: Anti-Defamation League, 1988), p. 41.

[27] Joseph P. Fried, "Howard Beach Defendant Given Maximum Term of 20 to 30 Years," *New York Times*, January 23, 1988, p. 1.

[28] *1987 Audit of Anti-Semitic Incidents*.

[29] Vivienne Walt, "A New Racism Gets Violent in New Jersey," *Newsday*, April 6, 1988, p. 4, part 11.

[30] Ibid.

[31] Timothy Egan, "Warriors of Hate Find No Homeland in Idaho," *New York Times*, January 2, 1988, p. 9.

[32] Jane Perlez, " 'Chaotic' State of School Halts Inspection Visit," *New York Times*, January 27, 1988, p. B1.

[33] Jane Perlez, "Knives and Guns in the Book Bags," *New York Times*, June 9, 1988, p. B1.

[34] Ibid.

[35] Ibid.

[36] Arnold H. Lubasch, "7 Convicted of Racketeering, 1 Acquitted in Westies Trial," *New York Times*, February 25, 1988, p. B1.

[37] Douglas Martin, "Love of Guns and Applause for Goetz," *New York Times*, April 25, 1988, p. B3.

[38] William E. Schmidt, "Pressure for Gun Control Rises and Falls, but Ardor for Arms Seems Constant," *New York Times*, October 25, 1987, p. E5.

[39] Ibid.

[40] Ibid.

[41] Sarah Lyall, "4 Charged With Beating Man to Death," *New York Times*, March 22, 1988, p. B1.

[42] "Three White Officers Charged With Texas Jail Murder," *New York Times*, March 6, 1988, p. 26.

[43] Don Terry, "2 White Police Officers Charged With Racially Motivated Assault," *New York Times*, March 1, 1988, p. B3.

44 Peter Applebome, "Killing Jars Dallas Into Taking Stock," *New York Times*, February 1, 1988, p. A18.

45 "National Prison Project Works to Eliminate Barbaric Conditions," *Civil Liberties* (ACLU Newsletter) fall 1987, p. 4.

46 Douglas Martin, "New York City Jails: System in Turmoil," *New York Times*, December 12, 1987, p. 33.

47 "Probe of Beating," *Newsday*, January 15, 1988, p. 16.

48 Clifford D. May, "Panel Hearings Will Examine Hate Crimes, *New York Times*, January 18, 1988, p. B1.

49 "Experts Say Mass Murders Are Rare But On Rise," *New York Times*, January 3, 1988, p. 16.

CHAPTER 2

1 Peter Stoler, *The War Against the Press: Politics, Pressure and Intimidation* (New York: Dodd, Mead & Company, 1986), p. 57.

2 Vicki Metz, "Newlywed Murder Strikes a Chord," *New York Times*, January 17, 1988, sec. 11, p. 1.

3 Todd S. Purdum, "Acts Linked to Increase in Bias Cases," *New York Times*, December 25, 1987, p. B1.

4 Walter Block, "Should TV Violence Be Censored?" *Free Press Network Newsletter*, vol. 4, no. 1, spring 1985, p. 4.

5 Marvin Kitman, "Defending Rivera on 'Death Row,' " *Newsday*, April 18, 1988, part 11, p. 9.

6 William J. McGuire, "The Myth of Massive Media Impact: Savagings and Salvagings," *Public Communication and Behavior*, vol. 1, 1986, p. 175.

7 Morris Janowitz, "Patterns of Collective Racial Violence," *The History of Violence in America*, a report to the Violence Commission, 1959, pp. 436–37.

8 Jeremy S. Weinstein, "The Media Have Wronged Howard Beach," *New York Times*, September 17, 1987, p. 26.

9 Ibid.

[10] Leslie Bennetts, "Do the Arts Inspire Violence In Real Life?" *New York Times*, June 26, 1985, pp. 1, 25.

[11] Ibid.

[12] David L. Bender and Bruno Leone, eds., *The Mass Media: Opposing Viewpoints* (St. Paul, Minn.: Greenhaven Press, 1988), p. 57.

[13] Donald MacGillis, *Crime in America, the ABC Report* (Radnor, Pa.: Chilton Book Company, 1983), p. 17.

[14] Sydney H. Schanberg, "The Brawley Case and Press Responsibility," *Newsday*, March 15, 1988, p. 63.

[15] "Violence in a Tube," ABC news program *Viewpoint*, show no. 1794, transcript in *Journal Graphics*, April 7, 1988.

[16] *Report of the National Advisory Commission on Civil Disorders* (Washington, DC: U.S. Government Printing Office, 1968), p. 203.

[17] *The Final Report of the National Commission on the Causes and Prevention of Violence to Establish Justice: To Insure Domestic Tranquility* (New York: Praeger Publishers, 1970), p. 71.

[18] Stephen B. Withey and Ronald P. Abeles, *Television and Social Behavior; Beyond Violence and Children* (Hillside, N.J.: Erlbaum Publishers, 1980), p. 237.

[19] David G. Clark and William B. Blankenberg, *Television and Social Behavior*, vol. 1 (Washington, DC: U.S. Government Printing Office, 1972), p. 113.

[20] *Attorney General Commission on Pornography Final Report* (Washington, DC: U.S. Department of Justice, 1986), p. 1263.

[21] Robert Baker and Sandra Ball, *Mass Media and Violence*, vol. IX, *A Report to the National Committee on the Causes and Prevention of Violence* (Washington, DC: U.S. Government Printing Office, 1969), p. 181.

[22] Bennetts, p. 25.

[23] Newsletter of the National Coalition Against Censorship, spring, 1988.

[24] *NCTV News*, vol. 8, no. 3–4, July–August 1987.

CHAPTER 3

[1] *NCTV News*, vol. 8, no. 7–8, November–December 1987.

[2] "U.S. Study Finds Violent Trend in Bestselling Fiction," press release of International Coalition Against Violent Entertainment, March 21, 1988.

[3] *Attorney General Commission on Pornography Final Report* (Washington, DC: U.S. Department of Justice, 1986), p. 1111.

[4] *NCTV News.*

[5] John Godwin, *Murder, USA: The Ways We Kill Each Other* (New York: Ballantine Books, 1978), p. 18.

[6] *World Almanac 1988.*

[7] Robert Baker and Sandra Ball, *Mass Media and Violence*, vol. IX (Washington, DC: U.S. Government Printing Office, 1969), p. 16.

[8] Peter Sandman, David M. Rubin, and David B. Sachman, *Media: An Introductory Analysis of American Mass Communication* (Englewood Cliffs, N.J.: Prentice Hall, 1976), p. 43.

[9] Stephen B. Withey and Ronald P. Abeles, *Television and Social Behavior: Beyond Violence and Children* (Hillside, N.J.: Erlbaum Publishers, 1980), p. 106.

[10] Donald MacGillis, *Crime in America, The ABC Report* (Radnor, Pa.: Chilton Book Company, 1983), p. 17.

[11] Baker and Ball, p. 20.

[12] Sandman, p. 411.

[13] David L. Bender and Bruno Leone, eds., *The Mass Media: Opposing Viewpoints* (St. Paul, Minn.: Greenhaven Press, 1988), p. 47.

[14] Ibid., p. 46.

[15] Clifford L. Linedecker, *Children In Chains* (New York: Everest House, 1981), p. 28.

[16] Andrea Dworkin, quoted in Walter Kendrick's *The Secret Museum: Pornography in Modern Culture* (New York: Viking, 1987), p. 228.

[17] Walter Kendrick, *The Secret Museum: Pornography in Modern Culture* (New York: Viking, 1987), p. 235.

[18] *The Meese Commission Exposed*, proceedings of the National Coalition Against Censorship. (New York: American Civil Liberties Union, 1986), p. 26.

[19] *Censorship News*, newsletter of the National Coalition Against Censorship, winter 1986, no. 23, p. 6.

[20] "U.S. Study Finds Violent Trend in Bestselling Fiction," press release of the International Coalition Against Violent Entertainment, March 21, 1988.

[21] *Attorney General Commission Final Report*, p. 1113.

[22] Ibid.

[23] D. M. Amoroso and M. Brown, *Technical Report of the Commission on Obscenity and Pornography*, vol. 8 (Washington DC: U.S. Government Printing Office, 1971), p. 216.

[24] *Censorship News*, NCAC newsletter, fall 1985, no. 22, p. 3.

[25] Newsletter of Morality in Media, vol. 26, no. 1, February 1987.

[26] Proceedings, NCAC, p. 18.

[27] *Censorship News*, NCAC newsletter, spring 1984, no. 17, p. 7.

CHAPTER 4

[1] *NCTV News*, vol. 5, no. 3–4, March–April 1984.

[2] Ibid.

[3] *The Final Report of the National Commission on the Causes and Prevention of Violence to Establish Justice: To Insure Domestic Tranquility* (New York: Praeger Publishers, 1970), p. 169.

[4] George Gerbner, *Television's Mean World: Violence Profile No. 14–15* (The Annenberg School of Communication: Philadelphia, 1986), p. 9.

[5] *Television and the Family*, pamphlet (Elk Grove Village, Ill.: American Academy of Pediatrics, 1986), p. 8.

[6] *The Final Report of the National Commission . . . ,* p. 169.

[7] Rose K. Goldsen, *The Show and Tell Machine* (New York: Dial Press, 1975), p. 8.

[8] *Television and the Family,* p. 8.

[9] George Comstock et al., *Television and Human Behavior* (New York: Columbia University Press, 1978), p. 80.

[10] Eric Mink, "Bum Rap for the Box: The TV Violence Theory Down the Tube," *Washington Journalism Review,* January/February 1982, p. 90.

[11] Gerbner, *Television's Mean World* . . . , p. 13.

[12] *The Final Report of the National Commission* . . . , p. 199.

[13] Surgeon General's Scientific Advisory Committee on TV and Social Behavior, *Television and Growing Up: The Impact of Televised Violence,* report to the Surgeon General (Washington, DC: U.S. Government Printing Office, 1972).

[14] David Pearl et al., *Television and Behavior: Ten Years of Scientific Progress and Implications for the Eighties,* vol. 1, National Institute of Mental Health project (Washington, DC: U.S. Government Printing Office, 1982), p. 16.

[15] "Where Do We Go From Here?", news report of the National Academy of Sciences, March 1983, unpaged.

[16] *NCTV News,* no. 7–8, November–December 1987.

[17] H. S. Eysenck and D. K. B. Nias, *Sex, Violence and the Media* (New York: St. Martin's Press, 1978), p. 89.

[18] Jerome L. Singer and Dorothy G. Singer, *Television, Imagination, and Aggression: A Study of Preschoolers* (Hillsdale, N.J.: Lawrence Erlbaum Associates, 1981), p. 80.

[19] George Gerbner, "Children's Television, A National Disgrace," *Pediatric Annals,* 14:12, December 1985, p. 822.

[20] The National PTA, *Parents, Children and TV: Highlights for Children* (Columbus, Ohio: 1984), p. 17.

[21] Stephen B. Withey and Ronald P. Abeles, *Television and Social Behavior: Beyond Violence and Children* (Hillsdale, N.J.: Lawrence Erlbaum Publishers, 1980), p. 13.

[22] Eysenck, p. 209.

[23] Jib Fowles, "The 'Craniology' of the 20th Century: Re-

search on Television's Effects," *TV Quarterly*, vol. XX, no. IV, 1984, p. 474.

[24] Paul Hirsch, "On Not Learning From One's Own Mistakes: A Reanalysis of Gerbner et al.'s Findings, Part II," *Communications Research Journal*, 8: 3–37.

[25] Jib Fowles, "Video Violence," *Houston Chronicle*, November 1, 1982, p. 468.

[26] Action for Children's Television, *TV and Teens: Experts Look at the Issues* (Reading, Mass.: Addison Wesley, 1982), p. 122.

CHAPTER 5

[1] Stephen Farber, *The Movie Rating Game* (Washington, DC: Public Affairs Press, 1972), p. 11.

[2] Ibid., p. 15.

[3] Ibid., p. 29.

[4] Roy Paul Madsen, *The Impact of Film* (New York: Macmillan, 1973), p. 272.

[5] Frank Manchel, *Gangsters on the Screen* (New York: Franklin Watts, 1978), p. 82.

[6] H. S. Eysenck, and D. K. B. Nias, *Sex, Violence and the Media* (New York: St. Martin's Press, 1978), p. 200.

[7] John E. O'Connor and Martin A. Jackson, *American History/American Film: Interpreting the Hollywood Image* (New York: Frederick Ungar Publishing Company, 1979), p. 60.

[8] Ibid., p. 62.

[9] John Fraser, *Violence in the Arts* (London: Cambridge University Press, 1974), p. 7.

[10] Arthur Asa Berger, *Film in Society* (New Brunswick, N.J.: Transaction Books, 1980), p. 57.

[11] John McCarty, *Splatter Movies, Breaking the Last Taboo of the Screen* (New York: St. Martin's Press, 1984), p. 146.

[12] J. Ronald Milavsky, *TV and Violence: A Study Guide* (Washington, DC: National Institute of Justice, 1986).

[13] John Godwin, *Murder, USA: The Ways We Kill Each Other* (New York: Ballantine Books, 1978), p. 16.

CHAPTER 6

[1] Katherine Bishop, "Access of Young to Dial-a-Porn Faces Challenge in West," *New York Times*, November 22, 1987, p. 26.

[2] Ibid.

[3] Vincent Canby, "At Home the Story's Different," *New York Times*, February 21, 1988, sec. 2, pp. 23, 29.

[4] *Attorney General Commission on Pornography Final Report* (Washington, DC: U.S. Department of Justice, 1986), p. 1416.

[5] *NCTV News*, vol. 8, no. 3–4, July–August 1987.

[6] John Rather, "A Cable Pioneer Sees a New Age of TV Dawning," *New York Times*, June 19, 1988, sec. 12, p. 2.

[7] Laura Mansnerus, "Rating Game: Parents Try to Fill Gap in Guidelines," *New York Times*, February 11, 1988, pp. C1, C10.

[8] *Clichés: Designed to Create Confusion Around the Problem of Pornography and Obscenity Law* (pamphlet) (New York: Morality in Media, no date.)

[9] *NCTV News*, vol. 8, no. 3–4, July–August 1987.

[10] New York City Bar Association, The Committee on Communications Law, "Content Regulation of Cable Television: 'Indecent' Cable Programming and the First Amendment," *ACLU*, March 5, 1986, p. 73.

[11] Ibid., p. 74.

[12] Ibid., pp. 82–83.

[13] Nathaniel C. Nash, "$1.2 Million Levied Over Sex Messages," *New York Times*, April 22, 1988, p. A12.

[14] Paul Schreiber, "Phone Utilities Seek to Pull Porn's Plug," *Newsday*, January 28, 1988, pp. 51, 63.

[15] Bishop, p. 26.

[16] Paul Schreiber, "Dial-a-Porn, Call Blocking General State, U.S. Friction," *Newsday*, June 28, 1988, pp. 35, 46.

CHAPTER 7

[1] *NCTV News*, vol. 8, no. 3–4, July–August, 1987.

[2] *Attorney General Commission on Pornography Final Report* (Washington, DC: U.S. Justice Department, 1986), p. 1387.

[3] Ibid., p. 48.

[4] Laura Mansnerus, "Rating Game: Parents Try to Fill Gap in Guidelines," *New York Times*, February 11, 1988, pp. C1, C10.

[5] *NCTV News*.

[6] Mansnerus.

[7] *NCTV News*.

[8] Dr. Victor Cline, *Psychologist Cites Porn's Effects on Children* (Salt Lake City: University of Utah Research, 1985).

[9] Mansnerus.

[10] "Growing Sadistic Entertainment Protested," press release of International Coalition Against Violent Entertainment, April 20, 1987, unpaged.

[11] *Attorney General Commission Final Report*, p. 937.

[12] *Clichés: Designed to Create Confusion Around the Problem of Pornography and Obscenity Law* (pamphlet) (New York: Morality in Media, undated).

[13] Ibid.

[14] *Attorney General Commission Final Report*, pp. 1056, 1057.

[15] Bill Van Haintze, "Post Student Charged With Rape, Sodomy," *Newsday*, June 2, 1988, p. 26.

[16] *Attorney General Commission Final Report*, p. 755.

[17] Clifford L. Linedecker, *Children in Chains* (New York: Everest House, 1981), p. 88.

[18] *Attorney General Commission Final Report*, p. 1040.

[19] Ibid., p. 1041.

[20] Philip Shenon, "Justice Department Plans Anti-Racketeering Drive Against Pornographers," *New York Times*, January 12, 1988, p. A16.

[21] Ibid.

[22] Ibid.

[23] *A Survey of Canadians' Attitudes Regarding Sexual Content*

of the Media, the La Marsh Research Programme, report no. 11 (Toronto: York University, 1985), p. 9.
24"Growing Sadistic Entertainment Protested."

CHAPTER 8

1 *NCTV Music Video Report*, December 1985, December 1986, July 1987.
2 "Los Angeles Citing Violence From Gangs, Adds Officers," *New York Times*, February 11, 1988, p. A21.
3 *NCTV Report.*
4 Ibid.
5 Ibid.
6 Pat Aufderheide, "Music Videos: The Look of the Sound," *Journal of Communications*, winter 1986, vol. 36, no. 1, p. 57.
7 Ibid., p. 58.
8 *NCTV Report.*
9 Tipper Gore, *Raising PG Kids in an X-Rated Society* (Nashville, Tenn.: Abingdon Press, 1987), p. 25.
10 David L. Bender and Bruno Leone. eds., *The Mass Media: Opposing Viewpoints* (St. Paul, Minn.: Greenhaven Press, 1988), p. 59.
11 Gore, *Raising PG Kids*, p. 50.
12 Ibid., p. 52.
13 Ibid., p. 53.
14 Ibid., p. 55.
15 Barry L. Sherman and Joseph R. Dominick, "Violence and Sex in Music Videos, TV and Rock 'n' Roll, *Journal of Communications*, winter 1986, vol. 36, no. 1, p. 79.
16 Ibid., p. 80.
17 Ibid., p. 80.
18 Aufderheide, p. 57.
19 Se-Wen Sun and James Lull, "The Adolescent Audience for Music Videos and Why They Watch," *Journal of Communications*, winter 1986, vol. 36, no. 1, p. 115.

[20] "Tipper Gore Widens War on Rock," *New York Times*, January 4, 1988, p. C18.

[21] Gore, *Raising PG Kids*, p. 75.

[22] Ibid., p. 76.

[23] "Tipper Gore Widens War on Rock."

[24] Gore, *Raising PG Kids*, p. 57.

[25] Bender, p. 124.

[26] Gore, *Raising PG Kids*, p. 76.

[27] David Hinckley, "Critics Say 'Rock' Is a 4-Letter Word," *New York Daily News*, January 12, 1987, p. 7.

[28] Gore, *Raising PG Kids*, p. 111.

[29] Ibid., p. 122.

[30] Bender, p. 131.

[31] *The Meese Commission Exposed*, proceedings of the National Coalition Against Censorship (New York: American Civil Liberties Union, January 16, 1986), p. 100.

[32] Bender, p. 129.

[33] Ibid., p. 130.

[34] Gore, *Raising PG Kids*, p. 149.

[35] *Censorship News*, newsletter of the National Coalition Against Censorship, April 1983, no. 13, p. 7.

[36] Gore, *Raising PG Kids*, p. 29.

[37] "Seating Changed For Rock Concerts," *New York Times*, December 13, 1987, p. 90.

SOURCES

NEWSPAPERS AND MAGAZINES

New York Daily News
"Critics Say 'Rock' Is a 4-Letter Word," Jan. 12, 1987.

Houston Chronicle
Jib Fowles, "Video Violence," Nov. 1, 1982.

Journal of Communications
"Music Videos: The Look of the Sound," 1986.
"Violence and Sex in Music Videos, TV and Rock 'n' Roll,"
    1986.
"The Adolescent Audience for Music Videos and Why
    They Watch," 1986.

New York Times
"The Age of Security," May 23, 1988.
"U.S. Says Violent Crime Dropped," May 9, 1988.
"Crime Reported to the Police Increased for 3rd Year,"
    April 17, 1988.

"A Week's Killings: A Profile of Violent Deaths in New York," April 8, 1980.

"Los Angeles Dragnet Over Gang Violence Leads to 634 Arrests," April 10, 1988.

"Three Youths Shot on a Subway Train in Brooklyn," April 6, 1988.

"Boy Convicted in Thrill Killing," March 12, 1988.

"Violence of Workplace: Unseen Signs, Unexpected Explosions," April 22, 1988.

"Two Homeless Men Set Afire by Youths at a Bus Terminal," January 20, 1988.

"Howard Beach Defendant Given Maximum Term of 20 to 30 Years," January 23, 1988.

"Warriors of Hate Find No Homeland in Idaho," January 2, 1988.

" 'Chaotic' State of School Halts Inspection Visit," January 27, 1988.

"Knives and Guns in the Book Bags," June 9, 1988.

"7 Convicted of Racketeering, 1 Acquitted in Westies Trial," February 25, 1988.

"Love of Guns and Applause for Goetz," April 25, 1988.

"Pressure for Gun Control Rises and Falls, but Ardor For Arms Seems Constant," October 25, 1987.

"4 Charged With Beating Man to Death," March 22, 1988.

"Three White Officers Charged With Texas Jail Murder," March 6, 1988.

"2 White Police Officers Charged With Racially Motivated Assault," March 1, 1988.

"Killing Jars Dallas Into Taking Stock," February 1, 1988.

"New York City Jails: System in Turmoil," December 12, 1987.

"Panel Hearings Will Examine Hate Crimes," January 18, 1988.

"Experts Say Mass Murders Are Rare But on Rise," January 3, 1988.

"Newlywed Murder Strikes a Chord," January 17, 1988.

"Acts Linked to Increase in Bias Cases," Dec. 25, 1987.

"Access of Young to Dial-a-Porn Faces Challenge in West," Nov. 22, 1987.

"At Home the Story's Different," Feb. 21, 1988.

"A Cable Pioneer Sees a New Age of TV Dawning," June 19, 1988.

"Rating Game: Parents Try to Fill Gap in Guidelines," Feb. 11, 1988.

"$1.2 Million Levied Over Sex Messages," Apr. 22, 1988.

"Justice Department Plans Anti-Racketeering Drive Against Pornographers," Jan. 12, 1988.

"Los Angeles Citing Violence From Gangs, Adds Officers," Feb. 11, 1988.

"Tipper Gore Widens War on Rock," Jan. 4, 1988.

"Seating Changed For Rock Concerts," Dec. 13, 1987.

"Heavy Metal, Weighty Words," July 10, 1988.

"Speed-Metal: Extreme, Yes; Evil, No," Sep. 25, 1988.

"Rap Music, Brash and Swaggering, Enters Mainstream," Aug. 29, 1988.

Newsday

"A New Racism Gets Violent in New Jersey," Apr. 6, 1988.

"Probe of Beating," Jan. 15, 1988, p. 16.

"Defending Rivera on 'Death Row,' " Apr. 18, 1988.

"The Media Have Wronged Howard Beach," Sep. 17, 1987.

"Do the Arts Inspire Violence In Real Life?" June 26, 1985.

"The Brawley Case and Press Responsibility," Mar. 15, 1988.

"Phone Utilities Seek to Pull Porn's Plug," Jan. 28, 1988.

"Dial-a-Porn, Call Blocking General State, U.S. Friction," June 28, 1988.

"Post Student Charged With Rape, Sodomy," June 2, 1988.

"Striking a Blow for Patrons," July 28, 1988.

PUBLICATIONS

ABC news program *Viewpoint.* "Violence in a Tube." Transcript, New York, Apr. 1988.

American Academy of Pediatrics. Pamphlet, *Television and the Family*. Elk Grove Village, Ill., 1986.

American Civil Liberties Union. Proceedings of the National Coalition Against Censorship. *The Meese Commission Exposed*. New York, January 1986.

American Civil Liberties Union. Newsletter, *Civil Liberties*. "National Prison Project Works to Eliminate Barbaric Conditions." New York, fall 1987.

American Civil Liberties Union. "Content Regulation of Cable Television: 'Indecent' Cable Programming and the First Amendment." New York, Mar. 1986.

Annenberg School of Communication. "Television's Mean World: Violence Profile No. 14–15." Philadelphia, 1986.

Anti-Defamation League. Special report, *The Hate Movement*. New York, 1986.

Anti-Defamation League. Summary report, *1987 Audit of Anti-Semitic Incidents*. New York, 1988.

Communications Research Journal. "On Not Learning From One's Own Mistakes: A Reanalysis of Gerbner et al.'s Findings, Part II." 1980.

Free Press Network Newsletter. "Should TV Violence Be Censored?" spring 1985.

International Coalition Against Violent Entertainment. "The 'Craniology' of the 20th Century: Research on Television's Censorship News." New York, fall 1985.

International Coalition Against Violent Entertainment. Press release, "U.S. Study Finds Violent Trend in Bestselling Fiction." New York, Mar. 1988.

International Coalition Against Violent Entertainment. Press release, "Growing Sadistic Entertainment Protested." New York, Apr. 1987.

Morality in Media. Newsletter. New York, Feb. 1987.

Morality in Media. Pamphlet, *Clichés: Designed to Create Confusion Around the Problem of Pornography and Obscenity Law*, New York, no date.

National Academy of Sciences. News report, "Where Do We Go From Here?" New York, Mar. 1983.

National Coalition Against Censorship. Newsletter, *Censorship News*, New York, Apr. 1983.

National Coalition Against Censorship. Newsletter, *Censorship News*. New York, spring 1984.

National Coalition Against Censorship. Newsletter. *Censorship News*. New York, winter 1986.

National Coalition Against Censorship. Newsletter, *Censorship News*, New York, spring 1988.

National Coalition Against Television Violence. *NCTV News*, July–Aug. 1987.

National Coalition Against Television Violence. *NCTV News*, Nov.–Dec. 1987.

National Coalition Against Television Violence. *NCTV Music Video Report*, Dec. 1985, Dec. 1986, July 1987.

National Coalition to Ban Handguns. Newsletter. Washington, DC, May 1988.

National Institute of Justice. *TV and Violence: A Study Guide*. Washington, DC, 1986.

National PTA. *Parents, Children and TV, Highlights for Children*. Columbus, Ohio, 1984.

Pediatric Annals. "Children's Television, A National Disgrace," Dec. 1985.

Public Communication and Behavior. *The Myth of Massive Media Impact: Savagings and Salvagings*. Vol. 1, 1986.

University of Utah Research. *Psychologist Cites Porn's Effects on Children*. November/December 1985.

Washington Journalism Review. "Bum Rap for the Box: The TV Violence Theory Down the Tube." Jan./Feb. 1982.

York University. The La Marsh Research Programme, Report No. 11. *A Survey of Canadians' Attitudes Regarding Sexual Content of the Media*. Toronto, July 1985.

BOOKS

Action for Children's Television. *TV and Teens: Experts Look at the Issues*. Reading, Massachusetts: Addison Wesley, 1982.

Amoroso, D. M., and M. Brown. *Technical Report of the Commission on Obscenity and Pornography*, vol. 8. Washington, DC: U.S. Government Printing Office, 1971.

Attorney General Commission on Pornography Final Report. Washington, DC: U.S. Department of Justice, 1986.

Baker, Robert, and Sandra Ball. *Mass Media and Violence*, vol. IX. *A Report to the National Commission on the Causes and Prevention of Violence*. Washington, DC: U.S. Government Printing Office, 1969.

Bender, David L., and Bruno Leone, eds. *The Mass Media: Opposing Viewpoints*, St. Paul, Minn.: Greenhaven Press, 1988.

Berger, Arthur Asa. *Film in Society*. New Brunswick, N.J.: Transaction Books, 1980.

Clark, David G., and William B. Blankenberg. *Television and Social Behavior*, vol. 1. Washington, DC: U.S. Government Printing Office, 1972.

Comstock, George, et al. *Television and Human Behaviors*. New York: Columbia University Press, 1978.

Currie, Elliott. *Confronting Crime: An American Challenge*. New York: Pantheon, 1985.

Eysenck, H. S., and D. K. B. Nias. *Sex, Violence and the Media*. New York: St. Martin's Press, 1978.

Farber, Stephen. *The Movie Rating Game*. Washington, DC: Public Affairs Press, 1972.

Fraser, John. *Violence in the Arts*. London: Cambridge University Press, 1974.

Godwin, John. *Murder, USA: The Ways We Kill Each Other*. New York: Ballantine Books, 1978.

Goldsen, Rose K. *The Show and Tell Machine*. New York: Dial Press, 1975.

Gore, Tipper. *Raising PG Kids in an X-rated Society*. Nashville, Tenn.: Abingdon Press, 1987.

Graham, Hugh David, and Ted Robert Gurr. *Violence in America: Historical and Comparative Perspectives*, Washington, DC: U.S. Government Printing Office, 1969.

Janowitz, Morris. "Patterns of Collective Racial Violence." *The History of Violence in America*. A report to the Violence Commission, 1959.

Kendrick, Walter. *The Secret Museum: Pornography in Modern Culture*. New York: Viking, 1987.

Kirkham, James F. *Assassination and Political Violence: A Report to the National Commission on the Causes and Prevention of Violence*. New York: Praeger Publishers, 1970.

Linedecker, Clifford L. *Children in Chains*. New York: Everest House, 1981.

MacGillis, Donald. *Crime in America, The ABC Report*. Radnor, Pa.: Chilton Book Company, 1983.

Madsen, Roy Paul. *The Impact of Film*. New York: Macmillan, 1973.

Manchel, Frank. *Gangsters on the Screen*. New York: Franklin Watts, 1978.

McCarty, John. *Splatter Movies, Breaking the Last Taboo of the Screen*. New York: St. Martin's Press, 1984.

National Advisory Commission on Civil Disorders Report. Washington, DC: U.S. Government Printing Office, 1968.

National Commission on the Causes and Prevention of Violence to Establish Justice, To Insure Domestic Tranquility; Final Report. New York: Praeger Publishers, 1970.

O'Connor, John E., and Martin A. Jackson. *American History/American Film: Interpreting the Hollywood Image*. New York: Frederick Ungar Publishing Company, 1979.

Pearl, David, et al. *Television and Behavior: Ten Years of Scientific Progress and Implications for the Eighties*. Washington, DC: U.S. Government Printing Office, 1982.

Sandman, Peter; David M. Rubin; and David B. Sachsman. *Media: An Introductory Analysis of American Mass Communication*. Englewood Cliffs, N.J.: Prentice Hall, 1976.

Singer, Jerome L., and Dorothy G. Singer. *Television, Imagination, and Aggression: A Study of Preschoolers*.

Hillsdale, N.J.: Lawrence Erlbaum Associates, 1981.

Stoler, Peter. *The War Against the Press: Politics, Pressure and Intimidation.* New York: Dodd, Mead, 1986.

Surgeon General's Scientific Advisory Committee on TV and Social Behavior. *Television and Growing Up: The Impact of Televised Violence.* Report to the Surgeon General. Washington, DC: U.S. Government Printing Office, 1972.

Withey, Stephen B., and Ronald P. Abeles. *Television and Social Behavior; Beyond Violence and Children.* Hillsdale, N.J.: Erlbaum Publishers, 1980.

World Almanac 1988.

FOR FURTHER INFORMATION

Corporation for Public Broadcasting
   (for teaching materials)
1111 16th Street NW
Washington, DC 20036
Attention: Douglas F. Bodwell, Director of Education
(202) 293-6160

Family Communications, Inc.
   ("Mr. Rogers' Neighborhood")
4802 Fifth Avenue
Pittsburgh, PA 15213
Attention: Toni G. Bednar, Director of Marketing Services
(412) 687-2990

ABC
1330 Avenue of the Americas
New York, NY 10019
Attention: Delores Morris, Director of Children's Programming
(212) 887-6934

CBS
51 West 52nd Street—33rd Floor
New York, NY 10019
Attention: Carolyn Ceslik, Director of Children's Programming

NBC
3000 North Alameda Avenue
Burbank, CA 91523
Attention: Phyllis Tucker Vinson, VP, Children's Programming

New Jersey Coalition for Better TV Viewing
P.O. Box 2382
Trenton, NJ 08607

American Academy of Pediatrics (task force statement)
141 Northwest Point Road
P.O. Box 927
Elk Grove Village, IL 60007
Attention: Jeff Molter, Media Manager
(312) 981-7871

Children's Institute International
    (children's welfare organization)
711 South New Hampshire Avenue
Los Angeles, CA 90005
Attention: Hasmik Sarkissian
(213) 385-5104

National Coalition on Television Violence
P.O. Box 2157
Champaign, IL 61820
Attention: Dr. Thomas Radecki, Chairperson
(217) 384-1920

University of Illinois at Chicago
    (extensive study on TV violence)

727 South Morgan
Chicago, IL 60607
Attention: Rowell Huesmann, Ph.D., Leonard Eron, Ph.D.
   (Psychology Department)
(312) 996-3036

Television Information Office ("TV Sets-in-Use")
   of the National Association of Broadcasters
745 Fifth Avenue
New York, NY 10022
Attention: Roy Danish, Director
(212) 759-6800

Children's Video Report
Woolworth Building—Suite 3715
233 Broadway
New York, NY 10279
Attention: Martha Dewing, Publisher/Managing Editor
(212) 227-8347

Broadcast Education Association (study by the
   Journal of Broadcasting & Electronic Media)
1771 N Street NW
Washington, DC 20036
Attention: L. Smith
(216) 672-2649

Annenberg School of Communication
University of Pennsylvania
Philadelphia, PA 19104
Attention: Robert Hornik, Associate Professor
   (Media Effects)
(215) 898-7041

Telecommunications Consumer Coalition
105 Madison Avenue—Suite 921
New York, NY 10016
Attention: Janice M. Engsberg, Ph.D., Executive Director
(212) 683-3834

Turner Broadcasting System
1050 Techwood Drive, NW
Atlanta, GA 30318
Attention: Linda Johnson, Director of Education Affairs

Media Action Research Center
475 Riverside Drive
Suite 1370
New York, NY 10115
Attention: Shirley Whipple-Struchen

Washington Association for Television and Children
P.O. Box 5642
Washington, DC 20016
Attention: Mary Ann Banta, President

Action for Children's Television
46 Austin Street
Newtonville, MA 02160
Attention: Mrs. Peggy Charren
(617) 527-7870

Media Relations Group W
888 Seventh Avenue
New York, NY 10106

International Reading Association
800 Barkdale Road
P.O. Box 8139
Newark, DE 19711

KIDSNET (A Computerized Clearinghouse for Children's
    Radio and Television)
6856 Eastern Avenue NW
Suite 208
Washington, DC 20012
(202) 291-1400

INDEX

Violence and the media
Berger, Gilda

13697
303.6 Ber

WATERLOO HIGH SCHOOL LIBRARY
1464 INDUSTRY RD.
ATWATER. OHIO 44201